Dishes for Two

100 Easy Small-Batch Recipes for Weeknight Meals & Special Celebrations

From the editors of

GOOD HOUSEKEEPING

HEARST
HOME

Contents

CHEESY TEX-MEX
CHICKEN PG. 68

Good Housekeeping celebrates the joy of sharing a meal.

Most of the recipes we publish serve four, six or even more people, which is great if you're feeding a big family. But if it's just you and someone else? Not so much.

Over the years, I've had so many people ask me if there was a simple way to scale down these recipes. Could they just divide the recipe in half and have it work? Sadly, the answer is no. That's why I'm so excited to bring you this collection of our favorite delicious recipes that our Test Kitchen team and I scaled down. So no matter what you're in the mood for, we've got you covered.

Happy cooking,

Kate Merker
Good Housekeeping Test Kitchen Director

If You're Craving Something...

QUICK & EASY (25 MINUTES OR LESS)
Pork Chops with Bloody Mary Tomato Salad page 61
Summer Squash & Pecorino Pasta page 55

ON THE LIGHTER SIDE
Cheesy Tex-Mex Stuffed Chicken page 68
Air-Fryer Mediterranean Chicken Bowls page 71
Apricot Grilled Pork Tenderloin & Peppers page 75

COMFORTING
Short Ribs with Creamy Polenta page 105
Vegan Queso page 195

SPICY
Spicy Sesame Sugar Snaps page 45
Spicy Bloody Mary page 175
Fiery Black Bean Soup page 103

Looking for something specific? Keep an eye out for these icons:

 Vegan Plant-based recipes that are free from meat, fish, eggs and dairy. Always read the labels on condiments to confirm that each ingredient actually is vegan! Opt for vegan wines and vinegars, as some traditional wines are processed in non-vegan ways.

 Vegetarian Make it meatless! You won't find fish, chicken, pork or beef here, but you will see recipes with dairy and eggs.

Heart-Healthy Based on our nutritionist's recommendations, these better-for-you recipes are lower in sodium, calories and saturated fat.

Chapter 1
Getting Started

Set yourself up for success by creating your grocery game plan, stocking your kitchen with the right tools and storing foods properly. Plus, discover delicious ways to give new life to the ingredients that inevitably land in the back of your fridge (and, two weeks later, in the trash).

Equip Your Kitchen

AIR FRYER This powerful countertop cooker will help you get tasty, crispy food on the table quickly. Its high-powered fan and top-down heat source work together to circulate hot air to quickly and evenly cook foods with little to no oil. It makes food crisp, tender and juicy. Plus, it's the ideal size for cooking for two!

BAKING SHEETS Invest in two sizes: Half sheet pans are ideal for sheet-pan dinners as well as for spreading out veggies while roasting so they crisp up nicely on the outside (rather than steaming in a crowded pan). Quarter sheet pans are practically meant for two-person cooking, whether you're making a protein or a side, and many fit in a toaster oven—plus, they're easier to clean than the larger pans.

ELECTRIC HAND MIXER Using an electric mixer ensures light and airy cake layers, fluffy whipped cream and icing that's velvety smooth—also, it's speedier and less tiring than endless stirring. But stand mixers often have a hard time with smaller quantities. A hand mixer is just the thing for quick mixing jobs and makes it easier to scrape the edges of the bowl so you can make sure you're reaching all the batter.

LOAF PAN From small-scale lasagnas and casseroles to brownies for two, this pan is good for much more than just making banana bread.

MEASURING CUPS For measuring dry ingredients, a standard set will keep you covered. For liquids, opt for a 2-cup measuring cup. It doesn't take up a lot of space and is great for smaller volumes of water or milk.

MEASURING SPOONS Look for a set that includes a 1/8 teaspoon and a 1/2 tablespoon. If the set doesn't have a 1/2 tablespoon, just keep in mind that 1 tablespoon is equal to 3 teaspoons, and 1/2 tablespoon equals 1 1/2 teaspoons.

MINI FOOD PROCESSOR Whether chopping nuts, fruits, herbs, vegetables or cheeses, this kitchen appliance can shave minutes off the prep time and doesn't take up a lot of counter space. And it's the perfect size for whipping up smaller batches of a dip like pesto or hummus using one can of beans.

MULTICOOKER No cooking tool is as versatile or foolproof as a multicooker (such as an Instant Pot). Most can brown food, pressure-cook, steam, slow-cook, make rice, ferment yogurt, hard-boil eggs and cook up creamy desserts. Best of all, you don't have to keep a close eye on it when it's on. It lets you whiz through meals that take longer on the stove, and cleanup is a breeze. The recipes in this cookbook will work with a smaller model or the standard 6-quart size.

RAMEKINS & MINI SKILLETS While deep casserole dishes are ideal for large-format dishes, ramekins and mini skillets fall on the other end of the spectrum. They're perfect for individually portioned pastas, soups, soufflés, egg bakes, desserts, you name it—and the ones with lids make freezing and reheating leftovers a snap. Pick up a few different sizes, if possible: 12-ounce ramekins will come in handy for the individual potpies on page 113 and the baked eggs on page 177; and 6- to 6 1/2-inch mini skillets are key to the brownies on page 199 and the fruit crumbles on page 205.

TOASTER OVEN Cook up smaller portions of food—or bake just one or two chocolate chip cookies at a time—without heating up your whole kitchen. Consider a model that doubles as an air fryer.

A NOTE ON ADJUSTING RECIPES

Many recipes serve four or more—and unfortunately, cooking for two doesn't always mean you can simply halve a recipe and hope for the best. You may have to pay extra attention to doneness cues (for example, "until golden brown"), adjust cooking times as needed or swap in different pots, pans and tools. You should also make sure you have enough oil in your pan to properly sear proteins: The Good Housekeeping Test Kitchen recommends using 1 tablespoon of oil whether you have two or four chicken breasts in your skillet. It all depends on the specifics of the recipe. The good news is, this cookbook is filled with recipes that are already perfectly portioned for two, so there's no math involved. All the guesswork has been eliminated! Once you master these tested-'til-perfect recipes, you can apply the small-batch cooking techniques you've learned from the Test Kitchen experts to some of your own beloved recipes.

Shopping Smarts

LOOK FOR THE LOOSE PRODUCE BINS
Buy exactly what you need—no more, no less. Instead of picking up a bag of green beans or a whole container of mushrooms, go to the section of the produce aisle where you can fill your cart with however much of each ingredient you need. The same rule applies to the bakery section, where you can buy individual hero rolls or demi baguettes instead of a package of six. The supermarket's salad bar is a great place to grab just a few cherry tomatoes, a handful of cucumber slices or a cup of peas.

BEFRIEND YOUR BUTCHER While it may be convenient to just grab a package of chicken breasts or ground meat and call it a day, it is not always efficient—more often than not you'll be stuck with too much meat. Instead, shop at your neighborhood or supermarket butcher and ask for the exact cut you want as well as the exact amount you need. (See if the butcher at a grocery store would be willing to split a package for you. It never hurts to ask!)

CHOOSE CHEESE WISELY You don't always need to buy the whole 8-ounce block of Cheddar. Check out the cheese counter, which will typically have a variety of size options available, as many stores cut up big wheels or blocks of cheese to package and sell on their premises. You may get lucky and find 4- or 5-ounce pieces. Dig through the odds-and-ends bin, where stores will stock all the random oddly shaped pieces of cheese that were too small to sell with the rest, usually at a discounted rate. Always opt for a whole piece so you can shred, slice or grate depending on the recipe.

SPLURGE (AND SAVE!) STRATEGICALLY
Sometimes it makes sense to spend more money. Exhibit A: A can of tomato paste costs around half of what you would spend on a tube of tomato paste, but will last in the fridge for a fraction of the time. (A can typically keeps for five days, whereas the tube can be refrigerated for up to eight weeks.)

SNAP A PIC Before you head to the store, use your phone to take a few pictures of your freezer and fridge. That way, when you're walking down an aisle and wondering if you need more butter or mayo, you won't buy items you already have "just in case" because you will be able to quickly refer to the pictures you took to confirm what you've got.

FILL YOUR FREEZER Picked at their peak and flash-frozen, frozen vegetables and fruits are often more nutritious than fresh, especially when fresh goods aren't in season. Plus, they won't go bad as quickly, making it easier to add just a cup to a recipe every now and then without having to brainstorm ways to use up the rest. You can also shop the freezer aisle for fresh frozen pastas like ravioli as well as shrimp, fish fillets, burger patties and frozen chicken breasts.

BE CAREFUL WITH BULK It is tempting to get two cartons of berries when they're on sale, but what's the value if you end up throwing one out? Instead, stock up on items that can be safely stored for the long haul. Think frozen seafood; nuts and seeds, which can last up to a year in the freezer; and eggs and some dairy, which can live in the fridge for three weeks or so. Crackers and cereals will stay fresh for a couple of months if they're unopened. Dried and canned beans and canned vegetables will keep almost indefinitely in a cool pantry.

SET UP A BUDDY SYSTEM Constantly finding that certain items are just way more cost-effective when bought in bulk? Ask a neighbor, family member or friend if they want to team up to shop with you and divvy up the goods. You can split the cost, share the savings and both make better use of the ingredients.

Maximize Your Groceries

When you can't find a smaller amount of an ingredient or it simply makes more sense to buy in bulk, try one of these techniques for ensuring that everything you buy will end up on your table—not in the trash.

PLAN With smaller-batch cooking, it's more important than ever to plan out your meals. Each week, think about what you want to cook and flag the most perishable ingredients in each recipe—fresh produce, herbs, dairy products, poultry, seafood. Prioritize selecting a recipe that also uses one (or more!) of those ingredients to cook for lunch or dinner another night that week. Sometimes it makes sense to select just one or two herbs to "spotlight" for the week so you won't be stuck with an assortment of wilted sprigs. Check out the meal-planning tips throughout this book—when you're facing a busy week, we have your back.

EXPERIMENT Missing an ingredient? Instead of running out to the store, brainstorm a simple substitution and get creative with your cooking! Swap in shallots for an onion, lemons for lime, Greek yogurt for sour cream, or one type of herb for another. When cooking, it's best to stick with ingredients similar to what the recipe originally called for, so replace one fresh herb with another, one variety of canned beans with another kind of beans or a splash of oil with a different type of fat. (PS: This rule doesn't apply to baking and desserts, as making those recipes is more of an exact science.)

FREEZE, FREEZE, FREEZE Use small freezer containers such as ice cube trays to make single-serving portions of leftover pasta sauce, pesto or chopped herbs (covered in olive oil). Toss 'em frozen straight into a hot pan for soups, pastas, sautés and more.

ROAST FOR THE MOST If you're staring at a refrigerator bin full of sad vegetables, grab a baking sheet and put them in the oven. They'll come out caramelized and tastier than you can imagine and will keep for a couple of additional days in the fridge. Add a protein, like salmon or chicken drumsticks, to make it a meal, or toss roasted vegetables into soups, salads and grain bowls.

MAKE A LIST Have a whiteboard near the fridge labeled "Danger Zone" on which you keep a running list of everything that is about to go bad. This will encourage you to find creative ways to cook with coconut milk or a jar of pesto rather than let it spoil and waste precious storage space.

TRACK IT If you shop in bulk, create a spreadsheet to track all the big purchases you make, adding a column in for "best by" dates. When it's time to meal plan for the week, sort the sheet by that column and prioritize brainstorming recipes that make use of any canned or frozen goods that will expire soon.

GO BIG (BATCH) Sometimes it's smartest to skip small-scale cooking altogether and meal prep instead. If you need to get through a ton of odds and ends, whip up a freezer-friendly stock, chili or soup.

GRILLED ROMAINE
LETTUCE WITH CREAMY
DILL DRESSING PG. 36

Storage Strategies

FOLLOW THE "FIRST IN, FIRST OUT" RULE
Stock each shelf of your fridge or pantry as if you worked at a supermarket. When unpacking your shopping bags, always put the newest boxes, cans and containers behind what's already sitting on the shelf. That way you will always reach for the older ones first.

FILL UP YOUR FRIDGE Use it wisely and you can keep root veggies, dairy and citrus on hand for weeks! Keep the fridge temperature between 35°F and 38°F. Fruit and veggies are best kept in the crisper drawer, which holds in humidity to keep items crisp. Dairy products and eggs should be kept on a shelf—not in the door, where temperatures are too warm. Use the door shelves to store condiments instead.

DON'T FREEZE AND FORGET The freezer should be your fallback, not a food cemetery. Make sure to label anything that goes in there with the date and a description of what it is. No, you will not automatically remember that the random plastic bag is Grandma's turkey chili in three months. You can also store bacon, chicken sausage, bread and nuts in the freezer to extend their shelf life.

KEEP HERBS FRESH Washing produce, including herbs, is crucial. To wash delicate herbs like basil and parsley, hold them by the stems and plunge the tops into cold water. Shake to dry, then place the stems in water like a bouquet. Leave basil uncovered and store it at room temperature; loosely cover well-dried parsley and cilantro with plastic and place in the fridge. For woody herbs like rosemary, thyme and oregano, swirl the sprigs around in cold water and spread them on a clean dishtowel to dry. Wrap the herbs in a slightly damp paper towel. This will keep the leaves protected and hydrated, helping them stay fresh longer. Store the bundles in an open plastic bag in your fridge's crisper drawer. Check for wilted pieces every few days and replace the paper towels as needed. Have a green thumb? Grow your own herbs.

REIMAGINE LEFTOVERS

While you can find ideas for using up specific ingredients throughout this cookbook, here are a few go-to ways to make the most of the odds and ends in your fridge:

Let's Do Lunch Pick up a container of greens or cook up a large batch of grains so you'll have a base ready for a variety of salads and grain bowls. Top with whatever ingredients are left from the night before—half a can of black beans, a scattering of corn kernels, half a pint of cherry tomatoes, or the remaining quarter of an onion. Since each midday meal will be using up ingredients originally intended for the same dinner, chances are everything will work together nicely. That said, use your best judgment and customize based on your own preferences. It is your lunch, after all!

From-the-Fridge Pizza Fridays As you plan out your meals for the week, leave one night free. Keep a stash of pizza dough in the freezer so you'll always be ready to whip up a pie at a moment's notice. Then take inventory of all the random ingredients in your fridge and choose a combination to top your pizza with. Get creative! Spread barbecue sauce on dough, then top with sliced red onion, pieces of chicken, half a bunch of cilantro, shredded Cheddar and frozen corn. Or opt for pesto or hand-crushed tomatoes topped with slices of grilled eggplant and zucchini, cannellini beans and dollops of ricotta. There are infinite possibilities. (Pro tip: Divide dough into individually sized portions so each person can customize their own personal pie.)

Brunch for Two The secret to cooking up a breakfast that will clear out the fridge and taste good? A carton of eggs. A few eggs take a half-wilted bunch of herbs, a quarter of an onion and a cup of canned corn from a waste of fridge space to a celebration-worthy brunch entrée such as a frittata or a quiche.

CHERRY TOMATO
CONFIT PG. 167

Chapter 2
Mix-and-Match Magic

Consider this your formula for 1,300 meal combinations, ready to customize based on the ingredients in your fridge or whatever you're craving on a given night. First you'll master the Good Housekeeping Test Kitchen's favorite way to cook most proteins and learn how to make a killer pan sauce—and 10 other sauces and condiments. Then there are 20 side dishes, including gluten-free and vegan options, so you can pick a protein, select a side and choose a sauce to top it all off. *Easiest dinners ever.*

Pick Your Protein

The secret to delicious steak, pork and chicken? Repeat this mantra: Sear, sear, roast.
Follow these steps to get a beautiful brown crust and the center cooked through just right.

SEAR

1. Pat the meat dry (extra moisture causes it to steam rather than sear) and let it sit at room temperature for 20 minutes.

2. Heat the oven to 400°F. Heat a 12-inch skillet (for the best crust, don't use nonstick) on medium-high. Season the meat evenly on both sides with salt and pepper, being extra generous with red meat.

SEAR

3. Add 1 tablespoon of olive oil to the hot skillet and swirl it to evenly coat the bottom of the pan. Add the meat and sear until the bottom is nicely browned (check the suggested cooking times on page 224).

4. Carefully flip each piece of meat and sear until the other side is browned too. Rotate the skillet to ensure even browning.

ROAST

5. Transfer the meat to a small rimmed baking sheet in a single layer (don't rinse the skillet yet!) and roast to desired doneness or, for chicken, until cooked through.

6. Transfer the meat to a cutting board and let rest for at least half its total cooking time to help it stay juicy and make it easier to slice. Don't forget to save any extra juices for the pan sauce!

Top It Off

Don't put your pan in the sink just yet! After searing meat, use your skillet to make a deliciously flavorful (and simple!) sauce.

1. Immediately after transferring your meat to the oven, start your sauce: Turn the heat to low. There should be about 2 tablespoons of fat in the pan. (In a 12-inch skillet, that's a thin, even coating on the bottom. If there's more, pour a little off. If there's less, add some olive oil.)

2. Add alliums (onions, shallots, leeks, scallions, garlic, etc.) and cook, stirring often, until slightly translucent and just tender, 2 to 3 minutes (do not let them brown).

3. Turn the heat to medium-high and add the vegetables. Season with salt and pepper and cook, stirring continuously, until just tender, 3 to 8 minutes.

4. Turn off the heat and add the liquid. (You want the heat off because the liquid will splatter when it hits the hot pan.)

5. Turn the heat to medium. Simmer, stirring and scraping bottom and sides of pan to incorporate any stuck brown bits into the liquid. Continue simmering and stirring until mixture is saucy, 3 to 4 minutes (this gives alcohol enough time to burn off and creamy sauces enough time to thicken).

6. Stir in any juices from the skillet and cutting board and season to taste. (If a sauce is too salty, stir in a bit of water. For a richer sauce, stir in a tablespoon of butter.) Scatter the fresh herbs all over the warm sauce before serving.

FAVORITE SAUCE COMBINATIONS

MUSHROOM WINE

- 1 leek, white and pale green parts only, cut into ¼-inch half-moons
- 14 ounces cremini mushrooms, quartered
- 1 cup dry red wine
- 1 teaspoon fresh thyme leaves

POBLANO CREAM

- 4 scallions, sliced
- 3 poblanos, seeded and chopped
- 1 cup heavy cream
- ¼ cup chopped cilantro

SPICY COCONUT

- 2 large shallots, thinly sliced
- 2 red Fresno chiles, seeded and sliced
- 1 cup coconut milk
- 1 tablespoon snipped chives

Pick a Sauce

A fresh sauce or tangy vinaigrette makes
a flavorful addition to any meal.

Herbed Tomato Vinaigrette

Make the most of in-season tomatoes by marinating them in herbs, sherry vinegar and olive oil. Serve over pasta, salad or grilled meats and vegetables.

Active Time 10 minutes | **Total Time** 10 minutes
Makes 2 cups

   1 small shallot, thinly sliced
   1 clove garlic, thinly sliced
   ¼ cup fresh basil, torn
   ¼ cup fresh parsley, torn
   ¼ cup 1-inch pieces fresh chives
   1 tablespoon fresh tarragon
   1 pound tomatoes (mix of sizes and colors), cherry tomatoes halved, large tomatoes cut into 1 ½-inch pieces
      Kosher salt and pepper
   ¼ cup sherry vinegar
   ¾ cup olive oil

To a pint-size mason jar, add the shallot, garlic, herbs, half the tomatoes and ½ teaspoon each salt and pepper. Add the vinegar, then the oil, and shake vigorously. Add the remaining tomatoes and shake again.

Per Serving (2 tablespoons)
About 95 calories, 10 g fat (1.5 g saturated fat), 0.4 g protein, 65 mg sodium, 1.4 g carbohydrates, 0.4 g fiber

Homestyle Italian Dressing

No need to stock your pantry with the bottled version when Italian dressing is this easy to pull off in a pinch. Toss it with salad greens or use it as a marinade.

Active Time 10 minutes | **Total Time** 10 minutes
Makes 1 cup

   3 tablespoons white wine vinegar
   1 tablespoon red wine vinegar
   1 clove garlic
   2 teaspoons Dijon mustard
   1 teaspoon honey
   ½ teaspoon red pepper flakes
      Kosher salt and pepper
   ⅔ cup canola or olive oil
   ¼ teaspoon dried oregano

In a blender, puree the vinegars, garlic, mustard, honey and red pepper flakes and ¼ teaspoon each salt and pepper until smooth. With the blender on high speed, gradually add the oil, then stir in the oregano.

Per Serving
About 170 calories, 19 g fat (1 g saturated fat), 0 g protein, 90 mg sodium, 2 g carbohydrates, 0 g fiber

---

TEST KITCHEN TIP

Toss 1 pound boneless, skinless chicken breast (cut into cubes) in ⅓ cup of the dressing. Marinate for at least 20 minutes and up to 1 hour. Thred onto skewers and grill.

Sriracha-Honey Vinaigrette

Whip up this quick dressing that's perfect for dipping crispy chicken nuggets, glazing seared pork and drizzling on slices of pizza.

Active Time 5 minutes
Total Time 5 minutes
Makes 3 tablespoons

   1 tablespoon cider vinegar
   1 tablespoon olive oil
   ½ tablespoon sriracha
   ½ tablespoon honey
    Kosher salt

In a bowl, whisk together all the ingredients with ⅛ teaspoon salt until smooth.

Per Serving
About 35 calories, 3.5 g fat (0.5 g saturated fat), 0 g protein, 100 mg sodium, 1 g carbohydrates, 0 g fiber

Mediterranean Olive Sauce

Briny bites are blended until smooth and brightened with lemon juice and mustard. Refrigerate, covered, for up to 5 days.

Active Time 5 minutes
Total Time 10 minutes
Makes 1 cup

- 1 cup pitted green olives
- ¼ cup olive oil
- 2 tablespoons fresh lemon juice
- 1 teaspoon Dijon mustard
- ¼ cup fresh flat-leaf parsley
- 2 cloves garlic
- ¼ teaspoon red pepper flakes

In a blender, puree all the ingredients until smooth.

Per Serving
About 90 calories, 9.5 g fat (1 g saturated fat), 0.3 g protein, 310 mg sodium, 1.4 g carbohydrates, 0.7 g fiber

Mojo Sauce

If you can't find sour oranges for this Cuban condiment you can substitute a 1:1 mixture of fresh lime and orange juices instead.

Active Time 5 minutes
Total Time 10 minutes
Makes 1 cup

- 4 large cloves garlic, pressed
  Kosher salt and pepper
- ¼ cup olive oil
- ⅔ cup sour orange juice (or ⅓ cup each fresh lime juice and fresh orange juice)
- ½ teaspoon dried oregano
- ½ teaspoon ground cumin

Place the garlic on a cutting board, sprinkle with ¾ teaspoon salt and use a knife to mash and scrape into a smooth paste. Add to a bowl along with the remaining ingredients and ¼ teaspoon pepper and stir to combine.

Per Serving
About 70 calories, 7 g fat (1 g saturated fat), 0.3 g protein, 180 mg sodium, 2.6 g carbohydrates, 0.2 g fiber

Mint Sambol

Packed with coconut, fresh mint and a hint of heat, this condiment pairs well with rice pilaf or grilled meats.

Active Time 5 minutes
Total Time 15 minutes
Serves 2

- ¼ cup unsweetened shredded coconut
- ½ jalapeño, chopped
- 1 clove garlic, chopped
- ⅛ small red onion, chopped
- ½ packed cup fresh mint leaves
- 1 tablespoon fresh lime juice
  Kosher salt

In a food processor, pulse the coconut, jalapeño, garlic and onion until combined, resembling fine crumbs and beginning to come together (add ½ tablespoon to 1 tablespoon water and scrape the sides if necessary). Add the mint and pulse to finely chop. Transfer to a bowl and stir in the lime juice and ¼ teaspoon salt.

Per Serving (2 tablespoons)
About 25 calories, 2 g fat (2 g saturated fat), 0.5 g protein, 85 mg sodium, 2.1 g carbohydrates, 1 g fiber

Ginger-Curry Yogurt Dressing

This do-it-all sauce shines as a marinade. The yogurt dressing slowly tenderizes the meat.

Active Time 5 minutes
Total Time 10 minutes
Makes 1 cup

- 1 clove garlic
- 1 1/2-inch piece fresh ginger, peeled and sliced
- 2 tablespoons fresh lime juice
- 1 cup plain yogurt
- 3/4 teaspoon ground turmeric
- 1/2 teaspoon curry powder
- 1/2 teaspoon sugar
- Kosher salt

In a blender, chop the garlic and ginger with the lime juice. Add the yogurt, turmeric, curry powder and sugar and 1/2 teaspoon salt and puree until smooth. Use as a marinade immediately (30 minutes for chicken and 15 minutes for shrimp) or let stand for 30 minutes before using as a dressing.

Per Serving (2 tablespoons)
About 20 calories, 1 g fat (1 g saturated fat), 2 g protein, 130 mg sodium, 2 g carbohydrates, 0 g fiber

Cilantro-Lime Yogurt

Use this creamy, citrusy sauce to flavor chicken salads or serve it alongside grilled fish or kebabs.

Active Time 5 minutes
Total Time 10 minutes
Makes 3/4 cup

- 1/2 jalapeño, seeded and chopped
- 1/2 cup plain Greek yogurt
- 1/4 cup fresh cilantro
- 1 tablespoon fresh lime juice
- 1/8 teaspoon ground cumin
  Kosher salt

In a blender, puree all the ingredients with 1/8 teaspoon salt until smooth.

Per Serving (2 tablespoons)
About 20 calories, 1 g fat (0.5 g saturated fat), 2 g protein, 50 mg sodium, 1 g carbohydrates, 0 g fiber

Roasted Red Pepper Relish

Taking a cue from Spanish romesco, this sauce makes nuts the star of the show.

Active Time 5 minutes
Total Time 10 minutes
Makes 1/2 cup

- 1/2 cup roasted red peppers
- 1/4 cup packed fresh flat-leaf parsley
- 2 tablespoons roasted salted almonds
  Kosher salt

In a mini food processor or blender, pulse all the ingredients with a pinch of salt until almost smooth.

Per Serving (2 tablespoons)
About 25 calories, 1.5 g fat (0 g saturated fat), 0.5 g protein, 65 mg sodium, 2 g carbohydrates, 1 g fiber

Lemon-Caper Salsa Verde

A secret ingredient brings an element of umami to the table: anchovies.

Active Time 5 minutes
Total Time 10 minutes
Serves 2

- 2 cups flat-leaf parsley
- 1/2 cup olive oil
- 2 tablespoons capers, rinsed
- 2 tablespoons finely grated lemon zest plus 1/4 cup lemon juice
- 2 anchovy fillets
- 1 small clove garlic

In a blender, puree all the ingredients, scraping down the sides as necessary, until smooth.

Per Serving (2 tablespoons)
About 130 calories, 14 g fat (2 g saturated fat), 0 g protein, 100 mg sodium, 2 g carbohydrates, 0 g fiber

TEST KITCHEN TIP

Enjoy it with chicken or shrimp, on sandwiches or tossed with pasta.

Choose Your Side

Round out your plate with roasted vegetables, cooked grains, a refreshing salad or another quick and easy side dish. Select a side based on what looks good to you, what's in season and how much time you have. If you're hoping to pair it with a sauce, choose something that has a similar flavor profile or includes a few of the same ingredients.

Sesame Cucumber Salad

This side salad is tangy, spicy, crunchy and as cool as a...well, you know. Choosing the right type of cucumber is important—it is the star ingredient, after all—as is learning the technique for salting the cucumbers. You won't want to skip the first step; it contributes to the overall flavor and texture of the salad. The cucumbers are also smashed, which helps trap extra dressing in all the misshapen pieces.

Active Time 5 minutes | **Total Time** 15 minutes

6 ounces Persian cucumbers

Kosher salt

2 teaspoons sesame oil

1 teaspoon sesame seeds

1 teaspoon low-sodium soy sauce

½ teaspoon lemon juice

½ teaspoon peeled and grated fresh ginger

½ teaspoon honey

2 tablespoons fresh cilantro, roughly chopped

Chile oil, for serving

1. Halve each cucumber lengthwise and, with the side of a chef's knife, bash it slightly to crush it, then cut each half into 4 to 6 chunks. Transfer the cucumbers to a bowl and toss with ¾ teaspoon salt. Let sit for 10 minutes.

2. Meanwhile, in a large bowl, whisk together the sesame oil, sesame seeds, soy sauce, lemon juice, ginger and honey.

3. Transfer the cucumbers to a colander and rinse, then shake off as much water as possible. Add to the bowl with the dressing and toss to combine, then toss with the cilantro. Serve drizzled with chile oil if desired.

Serves 2
About 70 calories, 5.5 g fat (0.5 g saturated fat), 1.1 g protein, 340 mg sodium, 5.2 g carbohydrates, 0.7 g fiber

Creamy Feta & Tomato Salad

You're going to want to drizzle this feta-yogurt sauce on everything after seeing what it does to this simple salad of raw tomato slices.

Active Time 25 minutes | **Total Time** 25 minutes

2 ounces feta cheese

1/4 cup whole-milk yogurt

1/2 clove garlic (pressed) plus 2 cloves garlic (very thinly sliced), divided

Kosher salt and pepper

1 pound heirloom tomatoes

1 1/2 tablespoons olive oil

1/2 tablespoon coriander seeds, lightly crushed

1/4 to 1/2 teaspoon hot paprika

1/4 cup fresh basil leaves

1. In a mini food processor, puree the feta, yogurt and pressed garlic and 1/8 teaspoon salt. Spread half the sauce on a plate. Slice the heirloom tomatoes, arrange half on the yogurt sauce and season with a pinch each of salt and pepper; repeat with the remaining sauce and tomatoes.

2. In a small skillet, cook the oil with the sliced garlic and coriander seeds on medium, stirring, until the garlic begins to brown lightly around the edges, 2 to 3 minutes. Add the paprika and a pinch of salt and cook for 1 minute more. Transfer to a bowl (the garlic will continue to cook). Spoon the oil mixture over the tomatoes and scatter on the basil.

Serves 2
About 230 calories, 18 g fat (6 g saturated fat), 7.8 g protein, 605 mg sodium, 12.6 g carbohydrates, 3 g fiber

---

ROASTED ASPARAGUS SALAD WITH FETA VINAIGRETTE

On a rimmed baking sheet, toss **1 pound asparagus** (trimmed) with **1 tablespoon olive oil** and **1/4 teaspoon each salt and pepper**. Arrange in a single layer and roast in a 425°F oven until the asparagus is lightly charred and just tender, 10 to 12 minutes. Meanwhile, in a food processor, puree **4 ounces feta cheese** and **1/4 cup whole-milk yogurt** until smooth. Spread half the mixture on a plate or platter. Arrange the asparagus on top of the feta mixture, top with **grated lemon zest** and serve with the remaining feta mixture.

Potato Salad with Vinaigrette

Ditch the heavy mayo-laden dressing and opt for a zippy red onion vinaigrette for this fresh spring side with green peas and dill.

Active Time 15 minutes | **Total Time** 30 minutes

1 pound baby yellow potatoes
Kosher salt and pepper
¼ medium red onion, finely chopped
1½ tablespoons white wine vinegar
1½ tablespoons olive oil
½ teaspoon Dijon mustard
¼ cup frozen peas, thawed
2 tablespoons fresh dill, roughly chopped

1. Put the potatoes in a pot and cover with cold water. Bring to a boil, add 1 teaspoon salt, reduce the heat and simmer until just tender, 12 to 15 minutes.

2. Meanwhile, toss the onion with the vinegar and ¼ teaspoon each salt and pepper and let sit, tossing occasionally.

3. Drain the potatoes and cool under cold water, then halve any that are large.

4. Whisk the oil and mustard into the vinegar mixture. Add the potatoes and toss to coat. Fold in the peas and dill.

Serves 2
About 275 calories, 10 g fat (1.5 g saturated fat), 5.3 g protein, 460 mg sodium, 45.8 g carbohydrates, 5.2 g fiber

Miso-Glazed Radishes

Compared to their raw counterparts, roasted radishes taste mellow, without that signature "bite." Here, the root vegetable is tossed with miso, a fermented soybean paste, and butter, adding a salty and luscious flavor.

Active Time 5 minutes | **Total Time** 25 minutes

1 tablespoon olive oil, divided

3/4 pound small to medium radishes, trimmed and halved, leaves reserved

1 tablespoon unsalted butter, at room temperature

1 tablespoon white miso

Sesame seeds, for serving

1. Heat the oven to 450°F. Coat a rimmed baking sheet with 1/2 tablespoon oil, then add the radishes, cut sides down, and drizzle with the remaining 1/2 tablespoon oil. Roast, rotating the baking sheet once, until the radishes are golden brown on the bottoms, about 15 minutes.

2. Meanwhile, in a medium bowl, combine the butter and the miso. Remove the radishes from the oven and transfer to the bowl. Toss until well coated, then fold in 1 cup radish leaves. Serve sprinkled with the sesame seeds.

Serves 2
About 150 calories, 12 g fat (4.5 g saturated fat), 2 g protein, 295 mg sodium, 10 g carbohydrates, 3 g fiber

MISO-CARAMEL DESSERT SAUCE

In a small saucepan on medium-low, combine 6 tablespoons **heavy cream** and 3 tablespoons **unsalted butter** (cut up), stirring, until melted. Whisk in 1 1/2 tablespoons **white miso** and 6 tablespoons **dark brown sugar**; cook, whisking, until slightly thickened and mixture coats the back of a spoon, 6 to 8 minutes. Use right away or refrigerate and rewarm before serving. Makes 1/3 cup.

Lemon Zucchini Orzo

Shake up your pasta salad routine this summer by tossing cooked orzo with shredded zucchini before adding a lemon vinaigrette, cheese and fresh herbs. Or sub in another pasta shape and try another flavor combination below.

Active Time 15 minutes | **Total Time** 30 minutes

4 ounces orzo

6 ounces zucchini, shredded (about 1 1/2 cups)

1/2 tablespoon grated lemon zest plus 1 1/2 tablespoons lemon juice

1/2 tablespoon olive oil

Kosher salt and pepper

1 1/2 tablespoons grated Parmesan

1/4 cup fresh basil, chopped

2 tablespoons roughly chopped fresh chives

1. Cook the orzo according to the package directions. Drain and immediately fold in the zucchini. Let sit for 1 minute.

2. Transfer the zucchini and orzo mixture to a bowl; toss with the lemon zest and juice, the oil and 1/8 teaspoon each salt and pepper and let cool completely.

3. Toss with the Parmesan, then fold in the basil and chives.

Serves 2
About 270 calories, 5.5 g fat (1.5 g saturated fat), 10 g protein, 200 mg sodium, 47 g carbohydrates, 3 g fiber

---

SWITCH IT UP

Choose your favorite noodles and cook, then mix in...

sautéed red onion slices + cooked crumbled bacon + halved cherry tomatoes
baby arugula + diced tomatoes + lemon zest + lemon juice + diced cucumber
chopped parsley + chopped mint + olive oil + canned cannellini beans
chopped roasted red peppers + sliced Spanish chorizo + olive oil + sherry vinegar

Grilled Romaine Lettuce with Creamy Dill Dressing

Romaine lettuce is an unexpected MVP on the grill. It gets a slightly smoky flavor from the hot grates. (See photo on page 15.)

Active Time 10 minutes | **Total Time** 15 minutes

1 ounce feta cheese

3 ½ tablespoons olive oil

1 ½ tablespoons nonfat plain Greek yogurt

1 tablespoon fresh lemon juice

½ small clove garlic

Kosher salt and pepper

1 ½ tablespoons packed fresh dill, chopped

1 romaine lettuce heart

1 ½ tablespoons roasted sunflower seeds

1. Heat a grill to medium.

2. In a blender or food processor, puree the cheese, oil, yogurt, lemon juice and garlic and a pinch each of salt and pepper. Transfer to a medium bowl; stir in the dill.

3. Cut the lettuce heart in half lengthwise; grill until charred in spots, about 2 minutes per side. Serve immediately, drizzled with the yogurt dressing and sprinkled with sunflower seeds.

Serves 2
About 300 calories, 29.5 g fat (5.5 g saturated fat),
5.2 g protein, 195 mg sodium, 5 g carbohydrates, 1.6 g fiber

TEST KITCHEN TIP

To make this a complete meal, throw salmon fillets or chicken breasts on the grill before charring up the lettuce.

Broccoli-Rice Pilaf

Instead of boiling in water, here rice is cooked in oil and aromatics first, resulting in a pilaf-style side.

Active Time 15 minutes | **Total Time** 30 minutes

½ tablespoon olive oil

½ onion, finely chopped

    Kosher salt and pepper

½ clove garlic, finely chopped

½ cup long-grain white rice

1 ¼ cups chopped
    broccoli florets

1. In a medium saucepan, heat the oil over medium. Add the onion, season with ¼ teaspoon each salt and pepper and cook, covered, stirring occasionally, until tender, 6 to 8 minutes. Stir in the garlic and cook for 1 minute.

2. Add the rice and stir to coat. Add 1 cup water and bring to a boil. Reduce the heat and simmer, covered, for 12 minutes. Add the broccoli and continue cooking until the rice is just tender, 3 to 5 minutes more. Remove from the heat and let stand, covered, until the broccoli is tender, about 5 minutes.

Serves 2
About 240 calories, 4 g fat (1 g saturated fat), 6 g protein, 255 mg sodium, 45 g carbohydrates, 2 g fiber

White Bean & Broccolini Salad

This dish can be made ahead and served at room temperature—ideal for nights when you want to pack up a picnic or just pull something from the fridge. It can easily be doubled too.

Active Time 20 minutes | **Total Time** 20 minutes

  Kosher salt and pepper

8 ounces Broccolini, trimmed (1 to 2 bunches)

1½ tablespoons olive oil

½ teaspoon grated lemon zest plus 1 tablespoon lemon juice

1 tablespoon honey mustard

¼ teaspoon red pepper flakes

1 tablespoon capers, drained and chopped

7 ounces canned small white beans, drained

1. Bring a medium pot of water to a boil and add a pinch of salt. Add the Broccolini and cook until the stalks are crisp-tender, about 2 minutes. Drain and transfer to an ice bath to cool. Drain and pat dry, then cut into large pieces.

2. In a large bowl, whisk together the oil, lemon zest and juice, mustard and red pepper flakes and ⅛ teaspoon each salt and pepper; stir in the capers. Add the Broccolini and the beans; toss to coat.

Serves 2
About 220 calories, 11 g fat (1.5 g saturated fat), 9 g protein, 565 mg sodium, 29 g carbohydrates, 9 g fiber

Farro with Tomatoes & Cucumber

This toothsome, slightly nutty grain is great as the base of a grain bowl (page 57) or served alongside a grilled steak (page 130). Here, it's livened up with fresh vegetables, herbs and an assortment of spices.

Active Time 25 minutes | **Total Time** 25 minutes

½ cup quick-cooking farro

1½ tablespoons olive oil

1 tablespoon red wine vinegar

½ clove garlic, pressed

¼ teaspoon ground cumin

¼ teaspoon ground coriander

⅛ teaspoon red pepper flakes

  Kosher salt and pepper

¼ small red onion, finely chopped

8 ounces tomatoes of mixed sizes and colors, cut into pieces

1 small seedless cucumber, cut into pieces

¼ cup fresh parsley leaves

1. Cook the farro according to the package directions.

2. Meanwhile, in a medium bowl, whisk together the oil, vinegar, garlic, cumin, coriander and red pepper flakes and ¼ teaspoon each salt and pepper.

3. Stir in the onion, then toss with the tomatoes and the cucumber. Fold in the farro and the parsley.

Serves 2
About 260 calories, 10.5 g fat (1.5 g saturated fat), 7.5 g protein, 285 mg sodium, 35 g carbohydrates, 4.5 g fiber

Brown Butter Brussels Sprouts

To add an aromatic nutty flavor to whatever you're making (mashed potatoes, Brussels sprouts, or pasta), cook butter until it melts, then foams, then turns pale brown.

Active Time 15 minutes | **Total Time** 30 minutes

12 ounces Brussels sprouts, halved

1 red onion, cut into ½-inch-thick wedges

2 tablespoons olive oil

Kosher salt and pepper

2 tablespoons unsalted butter

2 tablespoons sliced almonds

2 tablespoons golden raisins

1 tablespoon fresh lemon juice

1. Heat the oven to 400°F. On a quarter sheet pan, toss the Brussels sprouts, onion and oil, ½ teaspoon salt and ¼ teaspoon pepper. Turn the sprouts cut sides down and roast until golden brown and tender, 20 to 25 minutes.

2. Meanwhile, about 5 minutes before the Brussels sprouts are done, in a medium skillet, melt the butter on medium until foaming. Add the almonds and cook, stirring, until the almonds and butter are golden brown, 2 to 3 minutes. Add the raisins, the lemon juice and ¼ teaspoon salt and swirl in the pan to combine.

3. When the vegetables are cooked, transfer to a platter. Spoon the brown butter mixture over the Brussels sprouts and onions.

Serves 2

About 385 calories, 28.5 g fat (9.5 g saturated fat), 8.1 g protein, 770 mg sodium, 30.5 g carbohydrates, 8.6 g fiber

Coriander-Maple Glazed Carrots

This method for roasting vegetables results in crisp-on-the-outside cara-melized carrots every time. The secret: Because you preheat the baking sheet along with your oven, as soon as the carrots hit the heated surface they will start sizzling, not steaming (See photo on page 11).

Active Time 25 minutes | **Total Time** 55 minutes

12 ounces rainbow carrots, halved crosswise and thick ends quartered

1 tablespoon olive oil

3/4 teaspoon whole coriander seeds, crushed

Kosher salt and pepper

1/2 tablespoon maple syrup

1/2 teaspoon grated lime zest plus and tablespoon lime juice

1. Heat the oven to 450°F. Place a rimmed baking sheet in the oven.

2. Toss the carrots on the hot sheet with the oil, then add the coriander and 1/8 teaspoon each salt and pepper.

3. Roast, tossing after 15 minutes, until golden brown and tender, 15 to 20 minutes total. Immediately toss with the maple syrup and the lime zest and juice.

Serves 2
About 141 calories, 7 g fat (1 g saturated fat), 2.3 g protein, 250 mg sodium, 19.3 g carbohydrates, 4.7 g fiber

Chickpea Pasta Salad

This meal-prep-friendly side is made in a jar, so it's perfect to pack for picnics. Wait to flip the jar upside down until *right* before serving.

Active Time 10 minutes | **Total Time** 10 minutes

¼ very small red onion,
    finely chopped

2 tablespoons red wine vinegar

1½ tablespoons olive oil
    Kosher salt and pepper

½ cup canned chickpeas, rinsed

1 cup grape tomatoes, halved

2 tablespoons Kalamata
    olives, halved

1 cup cooked rotini pasta

1½ cups baby arugula

2 tablespoons crumbled
    feta cheese

In a 1-quart jar, shake onion, vinegar, oil and a pinch each of salt and pepper. Add chickpeas and gently shake to coat. Top with tomatoes, olives, pasta, arugula and feta. When ready to serve, turn upside down and let sit for 2 minutes so dressing can run over the rest of the ingredients. Can be prepared ahead and refrigerated for up to 2 days. Let stand at room temperature for at least 10 minutes before turning over to spread dressing.

Serves 1
About 650 calories, 31.5 g fat (6.5 g saturated fat), 19 g protein, 945 mg sodium, 72 g carbohydrates, 11 g fiber

Grilled Radicchio Slaw

Coleslaw doesn't have to be synonymous with creamy. Here, fresh pineapple is added to crunchy radicchio and the results are bright and flavorful.

Active Time 15 minutes | **Total Time** 25 minutes

  1 medium head radicchio

  1 tablespoon canola oil

  1 cup finely chopped fresh pineapple

  2 tablespoons packed fresh basil leaves, chopped

  1 tablespoon fresh orange juice

    Kosher salt and pepper

1. Heat a grill to medium. Cut the radicchio into quarters from the top to the bottom. Brush the cut sides with the oil. Grill on the cut sides, covered, turning once to the other cut sides, for 8 minutes total. Transfer to a cutting board to cool.

2. Slice the radicchio very thinly, then toss with the pineapple, basil and orange juice and 1/4 teaspoon each salt and pepper. Serve immediately or refrigerate, covered, for up to 1 day.

Serves 2

About 135 calories, 7.5 g fat (0.5 g saturated fat), 2.3 g protein, 265 mg sodium, 17.1 g carbohydrates, 2.3 g fiber

SWITCH IT UP

Replace the radicchio with thin wedges of red cabbage, the pineapple with ripe chopped mango and the basil with cilantro.

Spicy Sesame Sugar Snaps

Sear blanched sugar snap peas in a skillet to take them to the next level. They also make a great snack or mix-in for salads.

Active Time 15 minutes | **Total Time** 20 minutes

    Kosher salt

  8 ounces sugar snap peas, strings removed

  1 tablespoon toasted sesame oil

1 1/2 cloves garlic, chopped

 1/2 small red chile, thinly sliced, or 1/4 teaspoon red pepper flakes

  1 tablespoon red wine vinegar

    Chopped fresh parsley, for serving

1. Bring a medium pot of water to a boil; add a pinch of salt. Add the sugar snap peas and cook until almost tender, about 3 minutes. Drain well and transfer to a bowl of ice water. Let cool completely, then drain very well. Pat the peas dry.

2. In a skillet, heat the sesame oil, garlic and chile on medium-low and cook until the garlic is golden, stirring frequently. Add the peas and cook until just warm. Remove from the heat; stir in the vinegar and 1/4 teaspoon salt. Sprinkle with the parsley.

Serves 2

About 110 calories, 7 g fat (1 g saturated fat), 3 g protein, 250 mg sodium, 9 g carbohydrates, 3 g fiber

Air-Fried Potatoes with Bacon

Creamy potatoes, crispy bacon and a hint of fresh thyme make for a stellar side in the air fryer.

Active Time 15 minutes | **Total Time** 30 minutes

3/4 pound small new potatoes (about 16), halved

2 sprigs fresh thyme plus 1/2 teaspoon thyme leaves

1/2 tablespoon olive oil

Kosher salt and pepper

2 slices bacon

2 small shallots, cut into 1/4-inch wedges

1/2 tablespoon white or regular balsamic vinegar

1 teaspoon whole-grain mustard

1. In a medium bowl, toss the potatoes and thyme sprigs with the oil, 1/4 teaspoon salt and 1/8 teaspoon pepper. Add to the air fryer and top with the bacon. Air-fry at 400°F until the bacon is crisp, 6 to 12 minutes. Transfer the bacon to paper towels and let cool before breaking into pieces.

2. Shake the potatoes and continue to air-fry for 8 minutes. Add the shallots to the basket with the potatoes, toss to combine and air-fry until the vegetables are golden brown and tender, 8 to 12 minutes more.

3. Meanwhile, in a medium bowl, whisk together the vinegar, mustard and thyme leaves. Transfer the cooked vegetables to the bowl, adding any oil from the bottom of the basket, and toss to combine. Fold in the bacon.

Serves 2
About 290 calories, 14.5 g fat (4 g saturated fat), 7.2 g protein, 520 mg sodium, 35.7 g carbohydrates, 3.9 g fiber

Sweet & Spicy Sweet Potato Fries

Forget frying! Sliced sweet potatoes turn crispy in the oven—and you don't have to deal with splatters.

Active Time 15 minutes | **Total Time** 1 hour 15 minutes

1 tablespoon packed brown sugar

1/2 tablespoon olive oil

1/8 teaspoon ground cinnamon

Pinch of cayenne

Kosher salt and pepper

1 pound small sweet potatoes, cut into 3/4-inch-thick wedges

2 tablespoons grated Parmesan

1. Heat the oven to 375°F. In a medium bowl, combine the sugar, oil, cinnamon, cayenne and 1/4 teaspoon salt and 1/8 teaspoon pepper.

2. Add the sweet potatoes, sprinkle with 1 tablespoon Parmesan and toss to coat. Arrange the sweet potatoes on a large rimmed baking sheet in an even layer. Sprinkle with the remaining Parmesan and roast, rotating the pans halfway through cooking until deep golden brown and tender, 50 to 60 minutes.

Serves 2
About 210 calories, 6 g fat (2 g saturated fat), 6 g protein, 400 mg sodium, 36 g carbohydrates, 5 g fiber

BEEF & BROCCOLI
PG. 58

Chapter 3

Easy Weeknights

Refresh your recipe rotation with these, quick-to-fix dinners that will be on the table in 40 minutes (or less!). There are options to keep you satisfied year-round whether you're firing up the grill, trying out a new air fryer or craving a big bowl of pasta.

Chicken Mole Tacos

Taking a cue from Mexican mole sauces, a blend of dried chiles, spices and cocoa powder coats the chicken before it's roasted for the complex, layered flavor that is a signature of the more traditional dish.

Active Time 15 minutes | **Total Time** 25 minutes

3/4 pound boneless, skinless chicken breasts, cut into 1/2-inch pieces

3/4 teaspoon unsweetened cocoa powder

3/4 teaspoon ancho chile powder

1/2 teaspoon ground cinnamon
 Kosher salt and pepper

1/2 small red onion, thinly sliced

1/2 red pepper, thinly sliced

1/4 red cabbage, cored and thinly sliced

1 tablespoon fresh lime juice

4 small corn tortillas
 Cilantro and Greek yogurt, for serving
 Lime wedges, for serving

1. Heat the oven to 425°F. In a medium bowl, toss the chicken with the cocoa powder, chile powder and cinnamon and 1/4 teaspoon each salt and pepper. Transfer the chicken to a rimmed baking sheet and roast until cooked through, about 12 minutes.

2. Meanwhile, in another bowl, combine the onion, bell pepper and cabbage and toss with the lime juice and 1/4 teaspoon each salt and pepper.

3. Warm the tortillas, then fill with the chicken and top with the slaw as well as cilantro and yogurt if desired. Serve with the lime wedges.

Serves 2

About 360 calories, 6 g fat (1 g saturated fat), 39 g protein, 400 mg sodium, 38 g carbohydrates, 7 g fiber

---

TEST KITCHEN TIP

The quickest way to soft, pliable tortillas? Wrap a small stack in damp paper towels and microwave in 30-second increments. If you have more time, fire up the grill or heat them over an open flame on a gas stove: Turn the tortillas when small brown spots appear, transfer to a sheet of foil and wrap tightly.

Saucy Shrimp Curry

Transform frozen or fresh shrimp into a flavor-packed dinner with help from your spice drawer! Stock up on microwaveable basmati rice and this instantly becomes a one-pot meal.

Active Time 25 minutes | **Total Time** 25 minutes

1 tablespoon canola oil

1 medium shallot, thinly sliced

¼ teaspoon curry powder

¼ teaspoon ground cumin

¼ teaspoon black pepper

1 large clove garlic, finely chopped

⅓ cup ketchup

¼ teaspoon cayenne

Kosher salt

8 ounces large (26- to 30-count) peeled and deveined shrimp

Cooked basmati rice or toasted naan, for serving

Fresh cilantro leaves, for serving

1. Heat the oil on medium in a medium nonstick skillet. Add the shallot, curry powder, cumin and black pepper and cook, stirring occasionally, for 3 minutes. Add the garlic and cook, stirring, for 1 minute.

2. Add the ketchup, the cayenne and a pinch of salt and cook, stirring frequently, until thickened, about 2 minutes.

3. Add the shrimp and cook until just opaque, about 3 minutes. Serve with rice or naan and top with cilantro.

Serves 2 (curry only)
About 205 calories, 8 g fat (1 g saturated fat), 17 g protein, 1,155 mg sodium, 17 g carbohydrates, 1 g fiber

---

TEST KITCHEN TIP

You may know that a good ale or lager can ease the heat of a spicy meal. It turns out that wine can have the same effect. Choose a wine with lower levels of alcohol and tannins. Check the label for alcohol by volume (ABV); it should be 13% or under for red, 12% or under for white. Aromatic wines like Gewürztraminer and off-dry Riesling pair beautifully with this dish.

Summer Squash & Pecorino Pasta

If your garden is overflowing with fresh squash (or you want to shop seasonally in the summer), sauté this abundant vegetable in a skillet and then toss it with some pasta, cheese and mint for a fresh and easy dish.

Active Time 15 minutes | **Total Time** 25 minutes

6 ounces rigatoni

2 tablespoons olive oil

1 small shallot, halved and thinly sliced

3/4 pound zucchini and summer squash, thinly sliced into half-moons

Kosher salt and pepper

1 1/2 ounces Pecorino Romano cheese, grated

3 tablespoons fresh mint, thinly sliced

1/2 tablespoon fresh lemon juice

1. Bring a medium pot of water to a boil. Cook the pasta according to the package directions. Reserve 1/2 cup of the cooking liquid, then drain.

2. Meanwhile, in a large, deep skillet, heat the oil on medium. Cook the shallot, stirring occasionally, until golden brown, 3 to 4 minutes. Add the zucchini and summer squash and 1/4 teaspoon each salt and pepper and cook, tossing occasionally, until the squash is very tender but still holds its shape, 10 to 12 minutes.

3. Add the pasta to the skillet and toss with the squash and cheese, adding 1/4 cup of the reserved cooking liquid, to form a sauce that coats pasta; add more liquid if the pasta seems dry. Fold in the mint and lemon juice. Top with additional cheese and pepper if desired.

Serves 2
About 540 calories, 20.5 g fat (5.5 g saturated fat), 19.9 g protein, 500 mg sodium, 70 g carbohydrates, 5.9 g fiber

TEST KITCHEN TIP

Cook once, eat twice! Make double the squash mixture. Spread toast or grilled bread with ricotta cheese or top with fresh mozzarella and then spoon the squash mixture on top to serve for lunch tomorrow.

SWITCH IT UP

When it comes to grain bowls, the possibilities are endless: There are so many ways to mix up the base, toppings and sauces. Here are a few simple combinations to get you started:

basmati rice + sautéed kale and broccoli + sliced pan-seared steak
chopped scallions + teriyaki sauce

brown rice + sliced avocado + shredded red cabbage + carnitas
grated Monterey Jack cheese + salsa verde

quinoa + chopped cucumbers + grape tomatoes + grilled chicken + feta
tahini dressing

Crispy Tofu Bowls

Grain bowls make it possible to turn leftovers and odds and ends in the fridge into a delicious, easy-to-customize dinner so you have less food waste. Pro tip: Keep tofu on hand, as it lasts a little longer in the fridge than other proteins and is both budget-friendly and vegan-friendly.

Active Time 20 minutes | **Total Time** 30 minutes

1 14-ounce block extra-firm tofu

¼ small red onion, very thinly sliced

2 tablespoons red wine vinegar

2 tablespoons Thai sweet chili sauce

½ tablespoon olive oil

Kosher salt

½ seedless cucumber, chopped

3 tablespoons cornstarch

2 tablespoons canola oil

½ cup quinoa, cooked

1 tablespoon roasted cashew halves

Fresh parsley leaves, for serving

1. Slice the tofu ¼ inch thick and place between paper towels on a rimmed baking sheet. Top with a second baking sheet and place a cast-iron skillet or heavy cans on top to weigh it down for 10 minutes. Soak the onion in cold water.

2. In a medium bowl, whisk the vinegar, sweet chili sauce, olive oil and a pinch of salt. Pat the onion dry; toss with half the vinaigrette and the cucumber.

3. Sprinkle the tofu on both sides with cornstarch. In a 12-inch skillet, heat the canola oil on medium-high until hot. Carefully add the tofu. Cook until deep golden brown, 2 to 3 minutes per side. Drain on paper towels.

4. Divide the quinoa between two bowls. Top with the cucumber salad, cashews, parsley and tofu. Drizzle with the remaining vinaigrette.

Serves 2
About 625 calories, 32 g fat (3.5 g saturated fat), 27.6 g protein, 225 mg sodium, 56.3 g carbohydrates, 6.7 g fiber

Beef & Broccoli

This takeout-inspired dish's sauce is thickened with cornstarch. Substitute tamari for soy sauce to make it gluten-free. (See photo on page 48.)

Active Time 30 minutes | **Total Time** 35 minutes

3 tablespoons reduced-sodium soy sauce

1 tablespoon fresh lime juice

1 tablespoon packed brown sugar

1 clove garlic, grated

1/2 tablespoon peeled and grated fresh ginger

1/2 tsp to 1 teaspoon sriracha

1/2 teaspoon toasted sesame oil

1 1/2 teaspoons cornstarch, divided

1/2 pound flank or strip steak, halved lengthwise, then thinly sliced

1 small head broccoli (3/4 pound), cut into small florets, stems peeled (if necessary) and chopped

1 tablespoon canola oil

Cooked white rice, sliced red chiles, sesame seeds and scallions, for serving

1. In a medium bowl, whisk together the soy sauce, lime juice, sugar, garlic, ginger, sriracha and sesame oil and 1 teaspoon cornstarch. Transfer half to a small bowl and whisk in the remaining 1/2 teaspoon cornstarch and 3 tablespoons water; set aside.

2. Add the steak to the remaining sauce, toss to coat and let sit for 15 minutes.

3. Meanwhile, heat a large skillet on medium. Add 1/4 cup water and bring to a simmer. Add the broccoli and cook, covered, until bright green and just barely tender, 4 to 5 minutes. With a slotted spoon, transfer the broccoli to a plate.

4. Wipe out the skillet and heat the canola oil on medium-high. Add the steak in a single layer and cook until browned, 2 minutes per side. Add the sauce and simmer until beginning to thicken, 2 to 3 minutes. Add the broccoli and toss to combine.

5. Serve over rice and sprinkle with chiles, sesame seeds and scallions if desired.

Serves 2
About 355 calories, 17 g fat (4 g saturated fat), 30.8 g protein, 1,030 mg sodium, 22.2 g carbohydrates, 4.3 g fiber

Tofu Pad Thai

While traditional pad Thai is commonly made with fish sauce, this version skips it to keep the dish completely vegan.

Active Time 25 minutes | **Total Time** 35 minutes

½ 14-ounce block extra-firm tofu

1 tablespoon cornstarch

4 ounces rice noodles

2 tablespoons low-sodium soy sauce

1 tablespoon brown sugar

1 teaspoon sweet chili sauce

Juice of ½ lime

1 small clove garlic, grated

1 tablespoon canola oil

½ red bell pepper, sliced

1 cup bean sprouts

1 scallion, thinly sliced, plus more for serving

Chopped peanuts, for serving

Lime wedges, for serving

1. Bring a medium pot of water to a boil. Slice the tofu ½ inch thick and press for 10 minutes. Cut into cubes and toss with the cornstarch.

2. Meanwhile, cook the noodles in the boiling water according to the package directions, then rinse. In a small bowl, combine the soy sauce, brown sugar, sweet chili sauce, lime juice and garlic; set aside.

3. Heat the oil in a large nonstick skillet on medium. Add the pepper and cook until tender, 4 to 5 minutes. Remove from the skillet.

4. Add the tofu and cook, tossing, until golden brown, 4 to 5 minutes. Toss with the noodles and sauce. Fold in the pepper, bean sprouts and scallion; cook 2 minutes. Serve with the peanuts, the lime wedges and more scallions.

Serves 2

About 540 calories, 20 g fat (2.5 g saturated fat), 17.7 g protein, 605 mg sodium, 74.5 g carbohydrates, 3.9 g fiber

---

TEST KITCHEN TIP

Tofu is packed in water, so it's essential to press out the liquid or you'll be left with a flavorless, soggy mess. To do so, lay paper towels on a sheet pan. Open a package of extra-firm tofu and drain. Cut the tofu widthwise into slices and place on top of the paper towels in a single layer. Put more paper towels over the tofu, then top with another sheet pan. Place heavy objects on the sheet pan (think cans of tomatoes, a cast-iron skillet or cookbooks). Leave it alone for at least 30 minutes. Uncover, discard the paper towels and get cooking!

Pork Chops with Bloody Mary Tomato Salad

Bring happy hour to dinnertime by serving up a side salad inspired by the all-time favorite brunch cocktail (also on page 175). Fresh cherry tomatoes mixed with Worcestershire sauce, horseradish, hot sauce and celery are a great companion to a perfectly grilled piece of pork.

Active Time 25 minutes | **Total Time** 25 minutes

1 tablespoon olive oil

1 tablespoon red wine vinegar

1 teaspoon Worcestershire sauce

1 teaspoon prepared horseradish, squeezed dry

¼ teaspoon hot pepper sauce such as Tabasco

¼ teaspoon celery seeds

Kosher salt and pepper

½ pint cherry tomatoes, halved

1 stalk celery, thinly sliced

¼ small red onion, thinly sliced

2 small pork chops (1 inch thick; 1 to 1¼ pounds total)

2 tablespoons flat-leaf parsley, finely chopped

½ small head green-leaf lettuce, leaves torn

1. Heat a grill to medium-high. In a medium bowl, whisk together the oil, vinegar, Worcestershire sauce, horseradish, hot sauce, celery seeds and ⅛ teaspoon salt. Toss with the cherry tomatoes, celery and onion.

2. Season the pork chops with ¼ teaspoon each salt and pepper and grill until just cooked through, 5 to 7 minutes per side.

3. Fold the parsley into the tomatoes and serve over the pork along with the lettuce.

Serves 2
About 400 calories, 23 g fat (6 g saturated fat), 39 g protein, 525 mg sodium, 8 g carbohydrates, 3 g fiber

TEST KITCHEN TIP

Tiny light brown celery seeds are actually the fruit of a wild type of celery called smallage. Once dried, they pack a punch of concentrated flavor and are commonly used in pickling, stocks and coleslaws.

Ginger Pork & Cucumber Salad

While ground meat is great for meatballs, meatloaves and burgers, it really shines on a weeknight when it's simply cooked in a skillet, tossed with seasonings and sauces, then served over rice. No mixing, no shaping, no baking—just dinner on the table in 20 minutes.

Active Time 15 minutes | **Total Time** 20 minutes

1 tablespoon canola oil

8 ounces ground pork

1 clove garlic, finely chopped

½ small red chile, finely chopped

1 tablespoon plus 1 teaspoon peeled and grated fresh ginger, divided

2 tablespoons lime juice, divided

1 tablespoon low-sodium soy sauce, divided

½ teaspoon brown sugar

½ seedless cucumber, sliced

1 scallion, sliced

½ cup fresh cilantro

¼ cup fresh mint

Cooked rice, for serving

1. Heat the oil on medium-high until hot in a cast-iron skillet. Add the pork and cook until browned, breaking up with the back of a wooden spoon, about 7 minutes. Toss with the garlic, the chile and 1 tablespoon ginger. Remove from the heat and toss with 1 tablespoon lime juice and ½ tablespoon soy sauce, adding 2 tablespoons water if dry.

2. Whisk the remaining 1 tablespoon lime juice, ½ tablespoon soy sauce and 1 teaspoon ginger and the brown sugar. Toss with the cucumber and scallion; fold in the cilantro and mint. Serve with the pork over rice.

Serves 2 (salad only)
About 235 calories, 11.5 g fat (2 g saturated fat), 26.3 g protein, 370 mg sodium, 7.9 g carbohydrates, 2.1 g fiber

USE IT UP GROUND PORK

HOT 'N' SPICY PORK NOODLES Bring a medium pot of water to a boil and cook **4 ounces lo mein noodles** according to the package directions. In a small skillet, heat **1 teaspoon canola oil** on medium-high until hot. Add **4 ounces ground pork** and cook until browned, breaking up with the back of a wooden spoon, 5 to 7 minutes. Whisk together **1 tablespoon lower-sodium soy sauce**, **½ tablespoon balsamic vinegar** and **½ tablespoon sriracha**; add to the skillet with the pork along with **2 packed cups baby spinach**. Cook until the pork is cooked through and the spinach has wilted, stirring occasionally, about 2 minutes. Toss the pork mixture with the cooked noodles.

Salmon Burgers with Spiced Sweet Potato Fries

Looking to get more fish and seafood into your daily diet? Pulse salmon in a food processor and shape into patties for a delicious (and omega-3-packed!) substitute for beef in the classic burger-and-fries combo.

Active Time 25 minutes | **Total Time** 30 minutes

2 small sweet potatoes, cut into ½-inch-thick wedges

2 tablespoons olive oil, divided

½ teaspoon five-spice powder

Kosher salt

¾ pound skinless salmon fillet, cut into 1-inch pieces

1 tablespoon low-sodium soy sauce

½ teaspoon toasted sesame oil

1 scallion, thinly sliced

2 burger buns, toasted

½ avocado, thinly sliced

½ cup sprouts

1. Heat oven to 450°F. On a rimmed baking sheet, toss the sweet potatoes with 1 tablespoon olive oil, five-spice powder and ⅛ teaspoon salt. Roast until crisp, 20 to 25 minutes.

2. Meanwhile, in a food processor, pulse the salmon, soy sauce and sesame oil just until coarsely chopped. Add the scallion and pulse to combine. Form the mixture into two ¾-inch-thick patties.

3. Heat the remaining 1 tablespoon olive oil in a medium nonstick skillet on medium and cook the patties, turning once, until opaque throughout, 2 to 3 minutes per side. Transfer to the buns and top with the avocado and sprouts. Serve with the sweet potato fries.

Serves 2
About 600 calories, 27 g fat (4.5 g saturated fat), 42.6 g protein, 745 mg sodium, 47.2 g carbohydrates, 8.3 g fiber

TEST KITCHEN TIP
Pulsing small pieces of salmon a few times in a food processor helps the burgers stay together. But beware: Too much pulsing could make the mixture hard to form into burgers and could create a rubbery texture.

BBQ Chickpea & Cauliflower Pitas with Avocado Mash

These open-faced pitas just happen to be vegan—no need to source any alternative ingredients or omit something.

Active Time 20 minutes | **Total Time** 45 minutes

6 ounces cauliflower florets

1 tablespoon olive oil, divided

Kosher salt and pepper

7 ounces canned chickpeas, rinsed and drained

¼ teaspoon dark brown sugar

⅛ teaspoon ground cumin

⅛ teaspoon smoked paprika

⅛ teaspoon garlic powder

⅛ teaspoon chili powder

1 ripe avocado

1 tablespoon fresh lemon juice

2 flatbreads or pocketless pitas, toasted

1 tablespoon roasted salted pepitas

Hot sauce, for serving

1. Heat the oven to 425°F. On a rimmed baking sheet, toss the cauliflower with ½ tablespoon olive oil and ⅛ teaspoon salt; push to one side of the sheet.

2. Pat the chickpeas very dry with paper towels, discarding any loose skins. In a medium bowl, toss the chickpeas with the remaining ½ tablespoon olive oil, a pinch each of salt and pepper and the brown sugar, cumin, paprika, garlic powder and chili powder. Add to the other half of the baking sheet.

3. Roast the chickpeas and cauliflower until the cauliflower is tender and the chickpeas are crisp, 25 to 30 minutes.

4. Mash the avocado with the lemon juice and a pinch of salt; spread all over the flatbreads. Top with the roasted cauliflower and chickpeas and the pepitas. Serve with a drizzle of hot sauce.

Serves 2

About 500 calories, 25 g fat (4 g saturated fat), 11 g protein, 915 mg sodium, 65 g carbohydrates, 13 g fiber

---

USE IT UP CRISPY CHICKPEAS

Rinse the **remaining chickpeas**; pat very dry with paper towels, discarding any loose skins. On a rimmed baking sheet, toss with **½ tablespoon olive oil** and **⅛ teaspoon each kosher salt and pepper**. Roast at 425°F, shaking occasionally, until crisp, 30 to 40 minutes. Remove from the oven, transfer to a bowl and toss with **¼ teaspoon grated lemon zest**. Chickpeas will continue to crisp as they cool.

Cheesy Tex-Mex Stuffed Chicken

Chicken breasts are anything but boring when they're stuffed with a cheesy jalapeño-lime filling. (See photo on page 6.)

Active Time 20 minutes | **Total Time** 30 minutes

1 scallion, thinly sliced

1 jalapeño, thinly sliced

3/4 cup fresh cilantro,
1/4 cup chopped

1/2 teaspoon grated lime zest plus
1 1/2 tablespoons lime juice
and lime wedges for serving

2 ounces Monterey Jack
cheese, shredded

2 small boneless, skinless
chicken breasts

2 tablespoons olive oil, divided

Kosher salt and pepper

1 red or orange bell pepper
(or halves of 2), thinly sliced

1/4 small red onion, thinly sliced

3 cups torn romaine lettuce

1. Heat the oven to 450°F. In a bowl, combine the scallion, jalapeño, chopped cilantro and lime zest, then toss with the cheese.

2. Insert a knife into the thickest part of each chicken breast and move back and forth to create a 2 1/2-inch pocket that is as wide as possible without going through. Stuff the chicken with the cheese mixture.

3. Heat 1 tablespoon oil in a medium skillet on medium. Season the chicken with 1/4 teaspoon each salt and pepper and cook until golden brown on one side, 3 to 4 minutes. Turn the chicken and roast until cooked through, 10 to 12 minutes.

4. Meanwhile, in a medium bowl, whisk together the lime juice, the remaining 1 tablespoon oil and 1/4 teaspoon salt. Add the pepper and onion and let sit, tossing occasionally, for 10 minutes. Toss with the lettuce and the remaining 1/2 cup cilantro. Serve with the chicken and lime wedges.

Serves 2
About 360 calories, 22 g fat (7.5 g saturated fat), 32 g protein, 715 mg sodium, 10 g carbohydrates, 3 g fiber

---

TEST KITCHEN TIP

To tame the flame of fiery chiles and jalapeños, scrape off the seeds.

Crispy Pork Cutlets

These breaded cutlets are baked in the oven, so you can walk away for a few minutes or make a bright cabbage salad.

Active Time 20 minutes | **Total Time** 30 minutes

1 large egg

1 cup panko

1 tablespoon olive oil

8 ounces pork tenderloin, trimmed and cut into 4 pieces, then pounded to about 1/8 inch thick

Kosher salt and pepper

1 tablespoon rice wine vinegar

1 tablespoon fresh lime juice

1/2 tablespoon peeled and grated fresh ginger

1/2 teaspoon honey

1/4 small green cabbage (about 12 ounces), cored

1 scallion, thinly sliced on a diagonal

1. Heat the oven to 450°F. Beat the egg in a shallow bowl. In a second bowl or a pie plate, combine the panko and the oil.

2. Dip each pork cutlet in the egg, letting any excess drip off, then in panko, pressing gently to help it adhere; transfer to a rack set in a quarter sheet pan. Roast until golden brown and cooked through, 20 to 25 minutes. Sprinkle with 1/4 teaspoon salt.

3. Meanwhile, whisk together the vinegar, lime juice, ginger and honey and 1/4 teaspoon each salt and pepper.

4. Using a mandoline, thinly shave the cabbage. Toss in the vinaigrette, then toss with the scallion. Serve with the cutlets.

Serves 2
About 400 calories, 12 g fat (2.5 g saturated fat), 31 g protein, 680 mg sodium, 41.1 g carbohydrates, 4.5 g fiber

Air-Fryer Mediterranean Chicken Bowls

An air fryer doesn't just crisp wings and fries—this countertop star also makes it easy to whip up complete meals for two with minimal cleanup. In this recipe, chicken breasts cook up beautifully juicy and crispy with very little oil.

Active Time 15 minutes | **Total Time** 30 minutes

1 pound boneless, skinless chicken breasts, cut into 1 1/2-inch pieces

1 tablespoon olive oil

1 teaspoon dried oregano

1 teaspoon ground sumac
   Kosher salt and pepper

1 pint grape or cherry tomatoes

1 medium onion, roughly chopped

1 cup couscous

1 teaspoon grated lemon zest plus 1 tablespoon lemon juice, plus lemon wedges for serving

4 tablespoons fresh dill, divided
   Crumbled feta, for serving

1. In a large bowl, toss the chicken with the oil, then the oregano, sumac and 1/2 teaspoon each salt and pepper. Add the tomatoes and onion and toss to combine.

2. Arrange in an even layer in an air-fryer basket and air-fry at 400°F, shaking the basket occasionally, until the chicken is golden brown and cooked through, 15 to 20 minutes.

3. Meanwhile, in a medium pot, bring 1 1/4 cups water to a boil. Toss the couscous with the lemon zest and add to the boiling water. Stir, cover, remove from the heat, and let stand for 5 minutes. Fluff with a fork and fold in the lemon juice and 2 tablespoons of the dill.

4. Serve the chicken and vegetables over the couscous, spooning any juices collected at the bottom of the air fryer over the top. Sprinkle with the remaining 2 tablespoons dill and feta and serve with the lemon wedges if desired.

Serves 2
About 475 calories, 9.5 g fat (1.5 g saturated fat), 43 g protein, 425 mg sodium, 53 g carbohydrates, 5 g fiber

TEST KITCHEN TIP

No air fryer? Arrange the chicken, seasonings, tomatoes and onion on a baking sheet and bake at 425°F until the chicken is golden brown and cooked through, 15 to 20 minutes.

HOW TO BUY AND SERVE RAW TUNA

SHOP SMART

Go to a reputable market that has a knowledgeable staff and high inventory turnover. Even if you see the phrase "sushi grade," be aware that the term isn't regulated by the FDA. Let the fishmonger know you plan to eat your tuna raw.

GO (SUPER) FROZEN

When fish has been deep-frozen and stored per FDA regulations, any parasites have been killed. (But if you're concerned, the safest route is to cook seafood. Per the FDA, even freezing doesn't kill all harmful germs.)

KEEP IT COLD

Store it set over a bowl of ice in the fridge and use it the same day.

Ahi Tuna Poke Bowls

Poke is a marinated raw-fish dish that originated in Hawaii. It's typically served over rice, and you can add a bunch of tasty toppers like cucumbers, radishes, avocado and sesame seeds.

Active Time 20 minutes | **Total Time** 20 minutes

2 teaspoons low-sodium soy sauce

2 teaspoons toasted sesame oil

⅛ sweet onion, thinly sliced

1 scallion, thinly sliced

Kosher salt

8 ounces fresh ahi tuna, cut into 1-inch cubes

½ Persian cucumber, thinly sliced

½ tablespoon rice vinegar

⅛ teaspoon sugar

½ teaspoon black sesame seeds, plus more for sprinkling

½ ripe avocado, halved

Cooked rice, for serving

1. In a large bowl, whisk together the soy sauce, sesame oil, onion, scallion and a pinch of salt. Toss with the tuna and refrigerate until ready to use.

2. In a small bowl, toss the cucumber with the vinegar, sugar and sesame seeds and a pinch of salt. Let stand for 5 minutes.

3. Serve the tuna, marinated cucumbers and avocado over rice if desired. Sprinkle with additional black sesame seeds if desired.

Serves 2
About 265 calories, 13 g fat (2 g saturated fat), 30 g protein, 310 mg sodium, 8 g carbohydrates, 4 g fiber

---

USE IT UP AVOCADO

Mash the remaining ½ **avocado** with **lemon juice**, **salt** and **pepper**. Spread on **toast**, then top with **sliced tomatoes** and **everything seasoning**.

Apricot Grilled Pork Tenderloin & Peppers

Fire up the grill! Pork tenderloin cooks up beautifully on the grates and doesn't require many additional ingredients to become a satisfying supper.

Active Time 20 minutes | **Total Time** 25 minutes

2 peppers (red, yellow, orange or a combination), quartered

1/2 red onion, cut into 1/2-inch wedges

1 tablespoon oil

Kosher salt and pepper

1 small pork tenderloin (about 3/4 pound)

2 tablespoons apricot jam

1 tablespoon white wine vinegar

1. Heat a grill to medium-high. Toss the peppers and onion with the oil and season with salt and pepper.

2. Season the pork tenderloin with 1/8 teaspoon each salt and pepper. Grill the vegetables and the pork, covered, turning occasionally, until the vegetables are tender, 8 to 10 minutes. Transfer the vegetables to a cutting board.

3. Mix the jam and the vinegar in a bowl. Continue grilling the pork, basting with the sauce until cooked through (145°F), 3 to 6 minutes. Let rest for 5 minutes before slicing. Coarsely chop the peppers and serve with the onion, pork and any remaining sauce.

Serves 2
About 320 calories, 9 g fat (2.5 g saturated fat), 36 g protein, 335 mg sodium, 23 g carbohydrates, 3 g fiber

Pan-Fried Chicken with Lemony Roasted Broccoli

This dinner is a cinch to pull off in very little time. The secret: Pounding the chicken very thin (à la chicken Milanese or chicken paillard) allows the protein to cook through quickly.

Active Time 30 minutes | **Total Time** 30 minutes

12 ounces broccoli,
cut into florets

1 clove garlic, thinly sliced

2 tablespoons olive oil, divided
Kosher salt and pepper

2 6-ounce boneless, skinless
chicken breasts

½ cup all-purpose flour

½ lemon, halved lengthwise,
then thinly sliced crosswise

1 tablespoon fresh lemon juice

1. Heat the oven to 425°F. On a rimmed baking sheet, toss the broccoli and garlic with ½ tablespoon oil and ⅛ teaspoon each salt and pepper; roast for 10 minutes.

2. Meanwhile, pound the chicken breasts to an even thickness, season with ⅛ teaspoon each salt and pepper, then coat in flour. In a large skillet, heat 1 tablespoon oil on medium-high and cook the chicken until golden brown, 3 to 5 minutes per side. Nestle the chicken into the broccoli and roast until the chicken is cooked through and the broccoli is golden brown and tender, about 6 minutes.

3. Return the skillet to medium heat; add the remaining ½ tablespoon oil, then the lemon pieces, and cook, stirring, until beginning to brown, about 3 minutes. Add the lemon juice and 3 tablespoons water and cook, stirring and scraping up any browned bits. Spoon over the chicken and serve with the broccoli.

Serves 2
About 495 calories, 19 g fat (3 g saturated fat), 46.7 g protein, 365 mg sodium, 34.9 g carbohydrates, 5.1 g fiber

Oil & Vinegar Chicken Cutlet Sandwiches

Sandwiches are ideal whether you're looking to pack a picnic, transform your leftovers into something new or just get an all-in-one meal on the table in 20 minutes flat. Buy a demi baguette, and you won't have extra bread left behind (though that wouldn't be the worst thing in the world!).

Active Time 20 minutes | **Total Time** 20 minutes

¼ small red onion, thinly sliced

½ tablespoon red wine vinegar

Kosher salt and pepper

4 thin-sliced boneless, skinless chicken cutlets (about 8 ounces total)

1 tablespoon olive oil

3 cups baby spinach

2 5-inch pieces baguette, split and toasted

1. Toss the onion, vinegar and a pinch each of salt and pepper; let sit.

2. Heat the oil in a large skillet on medium-high. Season the chicken with ¼ teaspoon each salt and pepper and cook until browned and cooked through, 2 minutes per side; transfer to a cutting board.

3. Add the spinach to the skillet, season with salt and pepper and cook until just beginning to wilt, 1 to 2 minutes. Slice the chicken and sandwich it between the baguette halves with the spinach and onion.

Serves 2

About 395 calories, 10.5 g fat (1.5 g saturated fat), 34 g protein, 860 mg sodium, 38.8 g carbohydrates, 3.1 g fiber

---

GRILLED CHICKEN CAESAR BAGUETTE

Season **8 ounces boneless, skinless chicken breasts** with **¼ teaspoon each salt and pepper**, then grill to cook through. Let rest for at least 10 minutes before slicing. In a bowl, combine **2 tablespoons olive oil**, **½ tablespoon grated lemon zest**, **1 tablespoon fresh lemon juice**, **1 teaspoon Dijon mustard**, **1 teaspoon anchovy paste** and **½ ounce grated Parmesan**. Split **1 demi baguette** and spread the dressing on each side. Layer with the sliced chicken and **½ romaine heart** (torn into large pieces). Wrap in plastic and weigh down for at least 10 minutes.

Cod in Parchment with Orange-Leek Couscous

This oven-steaming method requires little oil or cleanup, making it an ideal way to get more seafood into your weekly rotation.

Active Time 15 minutes | **Total Time** 30 minutes

½ cup couscous

½ navel orange

½ leek (white and light green parts only), cut into ½-inch-thick half-moons

1 ½ cups baby kale

2 5-ounce skinless cod fillets

½ tablespoon olive oil

Kosher salt and pepper

1. Heat the oven to 425°F. Arrange two 12-inch squares of parchment on a baking sheet. In a bowl, combine the couscous with ⅓ cup water.

2. Cut the orange half in half, then peel one quarter and coarsely chop fruit. Fold the orange into the couscous along with the leek and baby kale.

3. Divide the couscous mixture among the parchment pieces; top each with a cod fillet. Drizzle with 1 tablespoon olive oil; sprinkle with ½ teaspoon salt and ¼ teaspoon pepper; squeeze the juice from the remaining orange quarter over the top.

4. Cover each with another piece of parchment; fold each edge up and under three times, tucking the edges underneath. Roast for 12 minutes.

5. Transfer each packet to a plate. Using scissors, cut an "X" in the center and fold back the triangles to serve.

Serves 2
About 340 calories, 5 g fat (1 g saturated fat), 32 g protein, 330 mg sodium, 40 g carbohydrates, 3 g fiber

---

PARCHMENT PACKETS 101

Roasting fish in paper pouches steams it with no fuss. Here's how:

1. Sandwich the ingredients between two square pieces of parchment paper. Fold each edge up and over three times.

2. Fold each corner of the packet under itself to create a seal that will remain intact while the packet is in the oven.

Air-Fried Steak Fajitas

Cook up sizzling steak fajitas without a single skillet.
The secret: your air fryer.

Active Time 15 minutes | **Total Time** 35 minutes

1 large red bell pepper,
  quartered lengthwise,
  then sliced crosswise

1 large yellow pepper,
  quartered lengthwise,
  then sliced crosswise

1 large red onion, sliced
  1/4 inch thick

2 teaspoons grated lime zest
  plus 2 tablespoons lime juice,
  plus lime wedges for serving

1/4 teaspoon ground cumin

1 tablespoon plus 2 teaspoons
  canola oil

1/2 teaspoon granulated
  garlic, divided

  Kosher salt and pepper

12 ounces skirt steak, cut into
  4-inch pieces, or hanger
  steak, halved

1 teaspoon ancho chile powder

1/4 cup fresh cilantro, chopped,
  plus more for serving

8 6-inch flour tortillas, warmed

  Sour cream, for serving

1. In a large bowl, toss the peppers, onion, lime zest and juice, cumin, 1 tablespoon oil, 1/4 teaspoon granulated garlic, 1/2 teaspoon salt and 1/4 teaspoon pepper. Air-fry at 400°F, shaking occasionally, 10 minutes.

2. Meanwhile, rub the steak with the remaining 2 teaspoons oil, then season with the ancho chile powder, the remaining 1/4 teaspoon granulated garlic and 1/2 teaspoon each salt and pepper. Push the vegetables to one side of the air fryer and add steak to the other side. Air-fry, flipping once, to desired doneness, 10 minutes for medium-rare.

3. Transfer the steak to a cutting board and let rest for at least 5 minutes before slicing. Toss the vegetables with the cilantro. Fill the tortillas with steak and peppers, then top with the sour cream, sprinkle with additional cilantro and serve with the lime wedges.

Serves 2
About 615 calories, 28 g fat (8 g saturated fat), 35 g protein, 1,500 mg sodium, 57 g carbohydrates, 6 g fiber

---

TEST KITCHEN TIP

No air fryer? Roast the vegetables on a baking sheet in a 425°F oven until tender, 10 to 12 minutes. Sear the steak in a skillet to desired doneness, 2 to 3 minutes per side for medium-rare.

Tex-Mex Pizzettas

Tortillas are one of the most versatile ingredients to have on hand—you can use them to make tacos, burritos, enchiladas, wraps or quesadillas. Here they become the base for a cheesy salad-topped pizza.

Active Time 10 minutes | **Total Time** 20 minutes

2 large flour tortillas

Canola oil, for brushing

½ 16-ounce can refried beans

2 tablespoons jarred salsa

½ ounce thinly sliced Spanish-style cured chorizo

½ cup coarsely grated pepper Jack cheese

Sliced avocado, shredded lettuce and chopped tomatoes, for serving

Lime wedges, for serving

1. Place a rimmed baking sheet in the oven and heat to 425°F. Lightly brush the tortillas with canola oil. Place the tortillas on the hot baking sheet and bake until crisp, 4 minutes per side.

2. Spread the refried beans on the tortillas, then spread ½ tablespoon jarred salsa on each. Divide the chorizo and cheese on top. Bake until the cheese melts, about 5 minutes.

3. Top the tortillas with avocado, lettuce and tomatoes. Squeeze fresh lime juice over the top.

Serves 2
About 550 calories, 29 g fat (10 g saturated fat), 21 g protein, 1,370 mg sodium, 57 g carbohydrates, 9 g fiber

---

USE IT UP JARRED SALSA

You can pair salsa with a bag of tortilla chips and call it a day—or take things to the next level and swap it in for canned tomatoes in your favorite Mexican-inspired recipes. For a super-quick way to finish off the leftover refried beans, salsa, chorizo and cheese from this recipe, stir everything into scrambled eggs.

Speedy Eggplant Parmesan

This deconstructed version of eggplant Parm will give you your fix without the need to bake (and freeze) a big casserole.

Active Time 20 minutes | **Total Time** 45 minutes

¼ cup all-purpose flour

1 large egg

½ cup panko

¼ cup grated Parmesan

¼ teaspoon garlic powder

　Kosher salt and pepper

½ tablespoon olive oil

½ small eggplant
　(about 6 ounces)

8 ounces cheese ravioli

½ cup marinara sauce, warmed

　Shredded fresh mozzarella,
　for serving

1. Heat the oven to 450°F. Bring a medium pot of water to a boil.

2. Place the flour on a plate. In a shallow bowl, beat the egg. In a second shallow bowl, combine the panko, Parmesan and garlic powder and ¼ teaspoon each salt and pepper, then stir in the oil.

3. Line a baking sheet with nonstick foil. Cut the eggplant into long ½-inch-thick sticks (reserve the other half for a future use). Coat the eggplant in flour, then in egg (letting any excess drip off), then in the panko mixture, pressing to adhere. Transfer to the prepared baking sheet and roast, turning halfway through, until golden brown, 15 to 18 minutes.

4. Meanwhile, cook the ravioli in the boiling water according to the package directions. Drain, divide between two bowls and top with the warmed marinara sauce. Cut the eggplant into pieces, then scatter on top of the ravioli. Top with the mozzarella if desired.

Serves 2
About 280 calories, 17 g fat (8 g saturated fat), 10.6 g protein, 350 mg sodium, 25.2 g carbohydrates, 2.5 g fiber

---

USE IT UP EGGPLANT

Turn leftover eggplant into a tasty pizza topping: In a large bowl, whisk together **1 tablespoon red wine vinegar**, **½ teaspoon honey** and **½ tablespoon olive oil**. Brush **½ small eggplant** (halved lengthwise), **½ red bell pepper** (quartered) and **1 plum tomato** (halved lengthwise) with **½ tablespoon olive oil** and season with **kosher salt** and **pepper**. Grill until tender, 2 to 4 minutes per side. Transfer to a cutting board and cut into large pieces; add to the bowl with the vinegar mixture, along with **½ tablespoon capers**, and toss to combine. Use to top pizzas.

White Bean & Tuna Salad with Basil Vinaigrette

Featuring budget-friendly proteins like canned tuna, eggs and beans, this salad will leave you feeling satisfied. The basil vinaigrette amps up the brightness, but you can sub in store-bought Italian dressing in a pinch.

Active Time 20 minutes | **Total Time** 25 minutes

Kosher salt and pepper

6 ounces green beans, trimmed and halved

2 large eggs

½ small shallot, chopped

½ cup fresh basil

1½ tablespoons olive oil

½ tablespoon red wine vinegar

¼ teaspoon pepper

2 cups torn lettuce

½ 15-ounce can small white beans, drained and rinsed

1 5-ounce can solid white tuna in water, drained

1. Bring a small saucepan and a large pot of water to a boil. To the large pot, add ½ tablespoon salt, then the green beans, and cook until tender, 3 to 4 minutes. Use a large slotted spoon to transfer the beans to a colander, then rinse under cold water to cool.

2. Use the slotted spoon to gently lower the eggs into the small saucepan of boiling water. Cook for 6 minutes. Transfer the eggs to a bowl of ice water and let them sit until the shells are cold to the touch. Peel the eggs and set aside.

3. Meanwhile, in a mini blender, puree the shallot, basil, oil and vinegar and ¼ teaspoon each salt and pepper.

4. Transfer half the dressing to a large bowl and toss with the green beans. Fold in the lettuce, beans and tuna and serve with the remaining dressing and the soft-boiled eggs.

Serves 2
About 340 calories, 16.5 g fat (3 g saturated fat), 31 g protein, 770 mg sodium, 24 g carbohydrates, 8 g fiber

---

TEST KITCHEN TIP

Double the dressing and toss with chopped cucumbers and ripe summer tomatoes or swirl into pasta salad.

PORK RAGU
RIGATONI PG. 117

Chapter 4

Scaled-Down Comfort

Casseroles, stews and soups don't always have to be for a crowd. These recipes are smaller versions of big-batch favorites, so you can dig into cozy dishes with hearty portions and nourishing ingredients with fewer leftovers.

French Onion Soup

Slow-cooking the onions until they're deep brown and caramelized gives this classic its distinctive flavor. Beef broth is traditional and amps up the richness, but you can sub in mushroom stock to make it vegetarian.

Active Time 50 minutes | **Total Time** 1 hour 50 minutes

2 tablespoons olive oil

2 pounds yellow onions
(2 to 3 large), thinly sliced

Kosher salt

¾ teaspoon all-purpose flour

2 tablespoons cognac
or dry white whine

1 32-ounce container
low-sodium beef broth

1 bay leaf

3 large sprigs fresh thyme,
plus more for sprinkling

½ tablespoon sherry vinegar

4 thin slices country bread

1½ ounces Gruyère cheese,
finely grated

1. Heat the oil in a medium heavy stockpot on medium. Add the onions and ¾ teaspoon salt, then reduce the heat to low and cook, stirring occasionally, until the onions are tender and have released their liquid, 10 minutes.

2. Increase the heat to medium-high and continue cooking, stirring often and scraping the bottom of the pot, until the onions are deep brown and caramelized, 40 to 50 minutes. If the bottom of the pot starts to get too dark, add 2 to 3 tablespoons water.

3. Sprinkle the onions with the flour and cook, stirring, for about 2 minutes. Stir in the cognac and cook for about 1 minute. Add the broth, bay leaf and thyme sprigs and simmer until reduced to about 4 cups, 18 to 20 minutes. Discard the herbs and stir in the vinegar.

4. When ready to serve, heat broiler. Arrange the bread on a rimmed baking sheet and sprinkle with the cheese and some additional thyme leaves. Broil in the top third of the oven until golden brown and bubbling, about 1 minute. Serve on top of the soup.

Serves 2
About 440 calories, 20 g fat (5.5 g saturated fat), 15 g protein, 1,255 mg sodium, 53 g carbohydrates, 8 g fiber

HOW TO SLICE AN ONION

Cut off the top and bottom of the onion. Slice in half through the root. Remove the skin. Cut into half-moons through the root.

Five-Spice Beef Stew

With vitamin-rich greens and colorful root veggies, this stew packs tons of fiber and flavor. To finish the 15- or 28-ounce can of crushed tomatoes, try the Short Ribs with Creamy Polenta on page 104.

Active Time 1 hour | **Total Time** 2 hours 30 minutes

1 pound boneless beef bottom round, trimmed and cut into 2-inch chunks

Kosher salt and pepper

2 tablespoons canola oil, divided

2 cups low-sodium beef broth, divided

2 medium shallots, quartered

2 small cloves garlic, peeled and finely chopped

1 1-inch piece ginger, peeled and finely chopped

1/2 teaspoon five-spice powder

2 star anise pods

1 small cinnamon stick

1 tablespoon tomato paste

6 ounces small carrots (about 3), peeled and chopped

6 ounces small parsnips (about 3), peeled and chopped

1 small purple-topped turnip, chopped

1 cup canned crushed tomatoes

1/2 large bunch spinach, thick stems discarded

1 tablespoon fish sauce

1/2 tablespoon lime juice

Fresh cilantro and thinly sliced red chile, for topping

1. Heat the oven to 325°F. Season the beef with 1/4 teaspoon each salt and pepper. Heat 1 tablespoon oil in a large Dutch oven on medium-high. Cook the beef, turning occasionally, until browned, 6 to 8 minutes. Transfer to a bowl.

2. Add 1/4 cup broth to the pot and cook, scraping up any browned bits, for 1 minute; transfer the juices to the bowl with the beef.

3. Lower the heat to medium and add the remaining 1 tablespoon oil to the pot along with the shallots and cook, stirring occasionally, until golden brown, 3 to 4 minutes. Add the garlic, ginger, five-spice powder, star anise and cinnamon and cook, stirring, for 2 minutes.

4. Stir in the tomato paste and cook for 1 minute. Return the beef and juices to the pot along with the carrots, parsnips, turnip and tomatoes and the remaining 1 3/4 cups broth. Bring to a boil, then cover and bake until the beef is very tender, 1 1/2 to 2 hours.

5. Remove from the oven and discard the star anise and cinnamon. Stir in the spinach, fish sauce and lime juice. Serve topped with cilantro and chile.

Serves 2
About 905 calories, 46 g fat (13 g saturated fat), 78.9 g protein, 2,215 mg sodium, 44.8 g carbohydrates, 11.4 g fiber

Tomato Soup with Parmesan Crostini

This sophisticated twist on the classic comfort soup-and-sandwich combo tastes way better than the kind with soup that comes out of a can. Craving a grilled cheese sandwich instead? Skip the Parmesan baguette slices and give our classic recipe a try.

Active Time 10 minutes | **Total Time** 1 hour 20 minutes

1½ pounds tomatoes

4 cloves garlic, smashed

½ red onion, thickly sliced

1 tablespoon olive oil

Kosher salt and pepper

Sliced baguette and finely grated Parmesan, for serving

1. Heat the oven to 325°F. On a quarter sheet pan, toss the tomatoes, garlic and onion with the oil and ¼ teaspoon each salt and pepper. Roast until the tomatoes are tender and juicy and the onion is tender, 60 to 70 minutes.

2. Transfer all the vegetables to a pot along with 2 cups water; bring to a boil, then remove from the heat. Using an immersion blender (or a standard blender), puree until smooth.

3. Increase the oven temperature to 450°F. Arrange the baguette slices on a quarter sheet pan, top with Parmesan and toast until the cheese melts; serve with the soup.

Serves 2
About 320 calories, 10.5 g fat (2.5 g saturated fat), 11.7 g protein, 710 mg sodium, 46.5 g carbohydrates, 5.5 g fiber

CLASSIC GRILLED CHEESE

Heat a medium nonstick skillet on medium. Spread **3 tablespoons mayo** on top of **four ½-inch-thick slices of bread**. Flip two pieces over and top with **4 ounces American or Cheddar cheese** (about 4 thin slices on each piece), then top with the remaining pieces of bread, mayo sides up. Add a **thin pat of unsalted butter** to the skillet, swirling to melt, then place the sandwiches in the skillet and cook until golden brown, 3 to 4 minutes. Flip, add another thin pat of butter and cook, pressing gently with a spatula, until the sandwiches are golden brown and the cheese has melted.

Instant Pot Chicken Pho

This Vietnamese noodle soup traditionally simmers away on the stove all day. This pressure-cooker version is ready in an hour.

Active Time 20 minutes | **Total Time** 1 hour

2 star anise pods

2 cloves

½ small cinnamon stick, smashed

½ teaspoon coriander seeds, crushed

¼ teaspoon black peppercorns

1 1-inch piece ginger, quartered and then smashed

¼ red onion, coarsely chopped

¼ Fuji apple

12 ounces chicken thighs, skin removed

1 tablespoon fish sauce, divided

1½ ounces instant rice noodles

Bean sprouts, sliced red chile, red onion, fresh mint or cilantro and lime wedges, for serving

1. Set an Instant Pot to Sauté. Add the star anise, cloves, cinnamon, coriander and peppercorns and sauté until fragrant, 3 to 4 minutes.

2. Add the ginger and onion and cook, stirring occasionally, for 4 minutes. Add the apple, the chicken, 3 cups water and ½ tablespoon fish sauce; cover and lock the lid. Cook on high pressure for 22 minutes. Use the natural-release method for 10 minutes, then release any remaining pressure.

3. Transfer the chicken to a plate. Strain the broth, discarding the remaining solids. Return the broth to the pot, add the noodles and let sit until tender, 3 to 4 minutes.

4. Meanwhile, shred the chicken, discarding the bones. Return to the pot and stir in the remaining ½ tablespoon fish sauce. Serve with desired toppings.

Serves 2
About 235 calories, 5 g fat (1.5 g saturated fat), 23 g protein, 730 mg sodium, 22 g carbohydrates, 0 g fiber

---

TEST KITCHEN TIP

No Instant Pot or other electric pressure cooker? In a large saucepan on medium, sauté the **star anise, cloves, cinnamon, coriander** and **peppercorns** until fragrant, 3 to 4 minutes. Add the **ginger** and the **onion** and cook, stirring occasionally, for 3 minutes. Add the **apple**, the **chicken**, **3 cups water** and **½ tablespoon fish sauce** and simmer until the chicken is cooked through, about 30 minutes. Follow the remaining recipe instructions.

Creamy Corn Chowder

The summertime soup has been rejiggered to use frozen instead of fresh corn and roasted root vegetables so you can enjoy a bowl at any time of year.

Active Time 25 minutes | **Total Time** 55 minutes

1 pound golden new potatoes, halved (quartered if large)

1 onion, cut into ¼-inch-thick wedges

1 tablespoon olive oil

3 sprigs fresh thyme

Kosher salt and pepper

2 cups low-sodium chicken broth

8 ounces frozen corn, thawed

2 tablespoons heavy cream

1 tablespoon fresh lemon juice

Crumbled cooked bacon, for serving

Thinly sliced scallions, for serving

1. Heat the oven to 450°F. On a rimmed baking sheet, toss the potatoes and onion with the oil, thyme and ¼ teaspoon each salt and pepper. Arrange all the potatoes cut sides down and roast until golden brown and tender, 25 to 30 minutes.

2. Discard the thyme from the vegetables and transfer half of them to a medium pot. Add the broth and bring to a boil. Using an immersion blender (or a standard blender), puree until smooth.

3. Add the corn and the remaining roasted vegetables to the pot and bring to a simmer. Stir in the cream, the lemon juice and ¼ teaspoon each salt and pepper. Serve topped with the crumbled bacon and scallions if desired.

Serves 2
About 445 calories, 15 g fat (5 g saturated fat), 13.6 g protein, 630 mg sodium, 72 g carbohydrates, 7.6 g fiber

---

TEST KITCHEN TIP

To cook up perfectly crisp bacon, place 6 pieces of bacon in a large skillet and add just enough water to cover. Cook on high until the water boils down, then reduce heat to low and cook bacon until crisp, turning often. Transfer to a paper towel-lined plate.

Fiery Black Bean Soup

Keep a few cans of beans, diced tomatoes and stock on hand so you'll always be minutes away from having a flavorful soup. To make this recipe vegetarian or vegan, swap in vegetable broth.

Active Time 45 minutes | **Total Time** 45 minutes

4 ounces tomatillos (about 2), halved

1 clove unpeeled garlic

1 medium yellow onion, cut into 1-inch-thick wedges

1 medium poblano, halved and seeded

1 small jalapeño, halved and seeded

1/2 tablespoon olive oil
Kosher salt and pepper

1/4 teaspoon ground cumin

1/4 teaspoon ground coriander

2 cups low-sodium chicken broth

1 15-ounce can low-sodium black beans, drained and rinsed

1/2 14.5-ounce can fire-roasted diced tomatoes, drained

1/2 small red onion, thinly sliced

1 tablespoon fresh lime juice
Fresh cilantro leaves, for serving

1. Heat the broiler. On a rimmed baking sheet, toss the tomatillos, garlic, yellow onion, poblano and jalapeño with the oil and 1/2 teaspoon each salt and pepper. Turn the peppers cut sides down and broil, rotating the pan every 5 minutes, until the vegetables are tender and charred, 15 minutes.

2. Discard the skins from the poblanos and garlic. Finely chop the vegetables and transfer to a Dutch oven. Add the cumin and coriander and cook on medium, stirring occasionally, for 2 minutes. Add the broth, beans and tomatoes and bring to a simmer, then cook for 4 minutes.

3. Meanwhile, toss the red onion with the lime juice and a pinch each of salt and pepper; let sit at least 10 minutes. Serve the soup topped with the pickled onion and cilantro.

Serves 2
About 325 calories, 6 g fat (1 g saturated fat), 20 g protein, 705 mg sodium, 53 g carbohydrates, 18 g fiber

---

USE IT UP FIRE-ROASTED TOMATOES

These tomatoes are charred over a flame before they're diced and canned, so they're smokier and more flavorful than straight-up canned tomatoes. Stir leftovers into homemade salsa, add to a pot of chili or mix into mac and cheese.

Short Ribs with Creamy Polenta

No other comfort food dish feels quite as celebratory as braised short ribs. Whatever the occasion, this delicious dish will make it memorable.

Active Time 40 minutes | **Total Time** 1 hour 50 minutes

1 pound bone-in beef short ribs
Kosher salt and pepper

2 tablespoons olive oil

1 small carrot, chopped

1 small stalk celery, chopped

1 medium onion, chopped

1 clove garlic, pressed

½ tablespoon tomato paste

6 tablespoons dry red wine

½ cup crushed tomatoes

¼ to ½ teaspoon
Worcestershire sauce

1 small sprig fresh rosemary

1 small sprig fresh thyme

¼ cup low-sodium chicken broth

1 cup whole milk

1 tablespoon unsalted butter
Kosher salt

⅓ cup polenta

2 tablespoons finely grated
pecorino cheese

1 tablespoon chopped
fresh parsley

1 tablespoon grated lemon zest

1 small clove garlic,
finely chopped

1. Pat the short ribs dry and season with a pinch each of salt and pepper. Set an Instant Pot to Sauté. Add the oil and brown the ribs, adding more oil if needed, about 6 minutes total; transfer to a bowl.

2. Add the carrot, celery, onion and garlic to the pot and cook, stirring often, until just tender, 6 to 8 minutes. Push the vegetables to the edges of the pot, add the tomato paste to the center and cook, without stirring, until browned, 1 to 2 minutes.

3. Add the wine and simmer until reduced, about 15 minutes. Stir in the crushed tomatoes, Worcestershire sauce, rosemary, thyme, broth and short ribs along with any juices from the bowl. Press Cancel. Lock the lid and cook on high pressure for 35 minutes. Use the natural-release method for 10 minutes, then release any remaining pressure.

4. Transfer the short ribs (and any loose bones) to a bowl; discard the rosemary and thyme. Skim off and discard any fat from the liquid. Using an immersion blender (or a standard blender), puree the sauce until smooth. Shred the meat into large chunks, discarding the bones, and stir back into the sauce.

5. In a small saucepan, bring the milk, butter and ¼ teaspoon salt to a boil. Whisk in the polenta. Cook, stirring constantly, until the mixture is thick and creamy and comes away from the side of the pan, 3 to 4 minutes. Stir in the cheese and, if too thick, 3 to 4 tablespoons water.

6. In a small bowl, mix the parsley, lemon zest and garlic. Serve the short ribs and sauce over polenta. Sprinkle with the gremolata.

Serves 2
About 915 calories, 65.5 g fat (28 g saturated fat), 36.1 g protein, 705 mg sodium, 46 g carbohydrates, 6.2 g fiber

Chicken Tikka Masala

This version of the Indian classic skips the marinade, meaning you can have a big bowl of the creamy tomato-based dish ready in less than 20 minutes. Pick up frozen rice or naan from the store so you'll have a super-easy side to round out the meal.

Active Time 10 minutes | **Total Time** 15 minutes

½ cup long-grain white rice

8 ounces boneless, skinless chicken thighs

3 tablespoons Greek yogurt

1½ teaspoons curry powder

Kosher salt

1 tablespoon unsalted butter

1 tablespoon peeled and chopped fresh ginger

2 small cloves garlic, chopped

¼ cup plus 2 tablespoons half-and-half

¼ cup canned tomato sauce

¼ cup fresh cilantro, chopped

Naan, for serving

1. Heat the broiler to high. Cook the rice according to the package directions.

2. Cut the chicken thighs into 1-inch chunks and pat dry with paper towels. In a bowl, toss the chicken with the yogurt, the curry powder and a pinch of salt. Arrange the chicken on a foil-lined quarter sheet pan; broil for 5 minutes.

3. In a 2-quart saucepan, cook the butter, ginger and garlic and a pinch of salt on medium, stirring, until the garlic is golden. Whisk in the half-and-half and tomato sauce. Stir in the broiled chicken. Bring to a simmer on high. Simmer, stirring, until the chicken is cooked through (165°F), about 5 minutes.

4. Serve the chicken and sauce over rice and top with cilantro. Serve with naan if desired.

Serves 2
About 425 calories, 19 g fat (10 g saturated fat), 26 g protein, 465 mg sodium, 36 g carbohydrates, 2 g fiber

Chicken, Sausage & White Bean Stew

Inspired by cassoulet, a rustic French dish loaded with a variety of smoked and fresh meats and sausages, this recipe maximizes minimal ingredients for a stick-to-your-ribs stew that tastes delicious and warms your soul.

Active Time 50 minutes | **Total Time** 2 hours 20 minutes

1 tablespoon olive oil

2 chicken thighs
(about 8 ounces)

Kosher salt and pepper

1½ links sweet Italian sausage
(about 4 ounces)

2 ounces bacon, cut into
½-inch pieces

¼ medium onion, finely chopped

½ medium carrot, finely chopped

¼ stalk celery, finely chopped

½ cup fresh breadcrumbs

1 small clove garlic, pressed

½ tablespoon fresh
thyme leaves

8 ounces canned cannellini
beans, drained and rinsed

½ cup low-sodium chicken broth

1. Heat the oven to 350°F. In a heavy medium saucepan, heat the oil on medium. Pat the chicken dry and season with a pinch each of salt and pepper. Place the chicken, skin side down, in the pan. Cook until golden brown, about 6 minutes. Turn and cook for 3 minutes more. Transfer to a plate.

2. Add the sausage to the pan and cook, turning until browned all over, 6 to 8 minutes. Transfer to a cutting board; let cool, then slice.

3. Add the bacon to the pan and cook, stirring occasionally, until golden brown and crisp, 8 to 10 minutes. With a slotted spoon, transfer to paper towels. Discard all but 1 tablespoon of fat in the pot.

4. Add the onion and a pinch of salt to the pot and cook, stirring occasionally, until golden brown and tender, 5 to 6 minutes. Add the carrot and celery and cook for 3 minutes more. Remove from the heat.

5. In a small bowl, combine the breadcrumbs, garlic and thyme and set aside.

6. Stir the beans and broth into the pan along with the chicken, sausage and bacon and sprinkle with the crumb mixture. Bake until the chicken is fork-tender and the stew has thickened, 45 to 60 minutes. Heat the broiler and broil until the crumbs are golden brown, about 3 minutes. Let stand for 10 minutes before serving.

Serves 2
About 565 calories, 33.5 g fat (9.5 g saturated fat), 34.2 g protein, 785 mg sodium, 29.4 g carbohydrates, 10 g fiber

---

FRESH BREADCRUMBS

Cut **1 thick slice country bread** into pieces and pulse in a food processor until coarse crumbs form.

Creamy Parmesan Risotto

Despite what you may have heard, there is no need to stand over the stove stirring patiently, waiting for perfectly cooked creamy rice as you slowly pour in simmering broth ladleful by ladleful. Just add all the broth at once and stir occasionally.

Active Time 15 minutes | **Total Time** 35 minutes

½ tablespoon unsalted butter

1 tablespoon olive oil

½ medium onion, finely chopped

1 clove garlic, finely chopped

¾ cup Arborio rice

Kosher salt and pepper

¼ cup dry white wine

1 ¾ cups low-sodium chicken broth

¼ cup finely grated Parmesan, plus more for serving

1. Heat the butter and oil in a large skillet on medium. Add the onion and cook, stirring occasionally, until tender, 6 to 8 minutes. Stir in the garlic and cook for about 2 minutes.

2. Stir in the rice and ½ teaspoon salt and cook, stirring occasionally, until golden brown and toasted, 4 to 6 minutes. Add the wine and cook until absorbed, about 1 minute.

3. Stir in the broth and simmer, stirring occasionally, until the rice is tender and creamy and the broth has been absorbed, 15 to 20 minutes. Stir in the Parmesan. Serve with additional Parmesan and cracked pepper.

Serves 2
About 445 calories, 15 g fat (5 g saturated fat), 14.2 g protein, 770 mg sodium, 65.2 g carbohydrates, 3.5 g fiber

---

SWITCH IT UP

With two or three more ingredients, you can transform the classic into something extra craveworthy:

Stir in **2 tablespoons pesto**, then top with a **fried egg**.

Fold in **1 ½ cups baby spinach**, then top with **1 sliced scallion**.

Stir in **⅓ cup frozen peas** (thawed), then top with **1 teaspoon lemon zest**, **¼ cup pea shoots** and **2 tablespoons fresh basil**.

Chicken and Sweet Potato Potpies

Individual ramekins come in handy for converting large-format dishes (like a classic chicken potpie) into scaled-down dinners.

Active Time 30 minutes | **Total Time** 55 minutes

1 tablespoon olive oil, plus more for the dishes

½ large onion, chopped

Kosher salt and pepper

8 ounces sweet potatoes, peeled and cut into ½-inch pieces

2 cooked boneless, skinless chicken breasts or rotisserie chicken breasts

2 tablespoons all-purpose flour

¼ cup dry white wine

1 cup low-sodium chicken broth

½ cup frozen peas, thawed

½ cup fresh flat-leaf parsley, chopped

½ tablespoon fresh tarragon, chopped (optional)

Pinch of freshly grated or ground nutmeg

½ sheet frozen puff pastry, thawed

1 large egg, beaten

1. Heat the oven to 375°F. Oil two 12-ounce (4-inch-diameter) ramekins.

2. Heat the oil in a medium skillet on medium heat. Add the onion and ¼ teaspoon each salt and pepper and cook, covered, stirring occasionally, for 6 minutes. Add the sweet potatoes and cook, covered, stirring occasionally, until tender, 8 to 10 minutes.

3. Meanwhile, shred the chicken (discarding skin and bones if using a rotisserie chicken).

4. Sprinkle the flour over the vegetables and cook, stirring, for about 1 minute. Gradually stir in the wine, then the broth, and bring to a boil. Add the chicken, peas, parsley, tarragon (if using) and nutmeg. Divide the mixture between the prepared ramekins. Place the ramekins on a rimmed baking sheet.

5. Using a 4-inch round cookie cutter, cut out 2 pieces of puff pastry. Place the pastry on top of the ramekins.

6. Brush the pastry with the egg and, using a sharp knife, cut 3 slits in the top of each piece of pastry. Bake until puffed and golden brown, 20 to 25 minutes.

Serves 2
About 835 calories, 43 g fat (8 g saturated fat), 53 g protein, 1,000 mg sodium, 57 g carbohydrates, 6 g fiber

PECORINO-EVERYTHING SPICE STRAWS

On a **floured** surface, unfold and roll **½ sheet puff pastry** (thawed) into a 5- by 8-inch rectangle. Brush with **1 beaten egg** and sprinkle with **¼ cup grated Pecorino Romano cheese**, then with **1 tablespoon everything seasoning**, lightly pressing to adhere. Cut the dough crosswise, into ½-inch-wide strips. Twist each strip and transfer to a parchment-lined baking sheet. Press the ends of the strips onto the parchment to prevent unraveling. Bake at 400°F until golden brown, 10 to 12 minutes. Let cool completely.

Ricotta Gnocchi with Toasted Garlic & Walnuts

It's a pasta-making party! DIY your own pillowy dumplings, then toss them with a delightful sauce (with only three ingredients!).

Active Time 20 minutes | **Total Time** 45 minutes

1 cup whole milk ricotta
(8 ounces)

1 large egg yolk

½ cup all-purpose flour, plus
1 to 4 tablespoons as needed

2 tablespoons finely grated
Parmesan, plus more for
serving

1 cup baby spinach, chopped

½ cup fresh basil, chopped

Kosher salt and pepper

1½ tablespoons olive oil

2 tablespoons walnuts,
roughly chopped

1 clove garlic, thinly sliced

1. In a medium bowl, combine the ricotta and egg yolk. Add ½ cup flour; the Parmesan, spinach and basil; and a pinch each of salt and pepper. Fold together to make a soft but not sticky dough; do not overmix. Fold in the remaining flour as needed.

2. Lightly flour a baking sheet. With lightly floured hands, roll the dough into 1 log, 1 inch wide and about 8 inches long. Cut the dough into 1-inch pieces; transfer to the prepared baking sheet and refrigerate, covered loosely in plastic, for 30 minutes.

3. Heat the oil in a medium skillet on medium. Add the walnuts and cook, stirring, 1 to 2 minutes. Add the garlic and cook, stirring, until the nuts are lightly toasted and the garlic is golden brown, about 1 minute. Remove from the heat.

4. Bring a medium pot of water to a boil; add ½ tablespoon salt, then the gnocchi, and cook until all have risen to the surface, 2 to 3 minutes, then 1 minute more. Using a large slotted spoon, transfer the gnocchi to the skillet with the walnuts, tossing gently to coat. Serve sprinkled with additional Parmesan.

Serves 2
*About 515 calories, 31.5 g fat (12 g saturated fat), 21 g protein,
370 mg sodium, 37 g carbohydrates, 2 g fiber*

USE IT UP MARSCAPONE

Spread mascarpone on toast, drizzle with honey and top
with sliced fruit (think nectarines, peaches or apples).

Shortcut Mac 'n' Cheese

Mascarpone cheese replaces the standard butter-and-flour combo in this super-fast creamy stovetop mac.

Active Time 15 minutes | **Total Time** 35 minutes

  3 slices bacon
  1 medium sweet potato (about 8 ounces),
    peeled and cut into 3/4-inch pieces
  1 tablespoon olive oil
  1 teaspoon fresh thyme,
    plus more for serving
    Kosher salt and pepper
  6 ounces mezzi or regular rigatoni
  ¼ cup mascarpone cheese
  1½ ounces extra-sharp Cheddar, finely grated

1. Heat the oven to 450°F. On one quarter sheet pan, arrange the bacon. On another quarter sheet pan, toss the sweet potato with the olive oil, the thyme and ¼ teaspoon each salt and pepper. Roast the bacon until browned, 12 to 15 minutes. Roast the sweet potato for 12 minutes, then stir and cook until golden brown, 6 to 9 minutes more. Break the cooled bacon into pieces.

2. Cook the pasta according to the package directions, reserving ½ cup cooking water before draining. Drain the pasta; return to the pot and toss with the mascarpone cheese and Cheddar until melted, adding reserved pasta water as needed. Fold in the sweet potato and the bacon; garnish with thyme.

Serves 2
About 505 calories, 29.5 g fat (14.5 g saturated fat), 17.4 g protein, 625 mg sodium, 41.9 g carbohydrates, 3.6 g fiber

Pork Ragu Rigatoni

There's nothing more comforting than a big bowl of pasta. (See photo on page 88.)

Active Time 50 minutes | **Total Time** 50 minutes

  6 ounces rigatoni
    Kosher salt and pepper
  1 tablespoon olive oil
  1 small clove garlic, finely chopped
 12 ounces ground pork
  3 tablespoons tomato paste
  ½ cup dry white wine
  ¼ cup flat-leaf parsley, roughly chopped
    Shaved ricotta salata, for serving (optional)

1. Cook the pasta according to the package directions.

2. Meanwhile, in a large skillet, heat the oil and garlic on medium for 30 seconds. Add the pork, season with a pinch each of salt and pepper and cook, breaking the pork into pieces, until no longer pink, 5 to 6 minutes.

3. Add the tomato paste and cook, stirring, for 2 minutes. Add the wine and simmer until it no longer smells like wine, about 3 minutes. Stir in the parsley. Drain the pasta and toss with the ragu. Serve with ricotta salata if desired.

Serves 2
About 615 calories, 26.5 g fat (7.5 g saturated fat), 33 g protein, 550 mg sodium, 59 g carbohydrates, 3 g fiber

Loaf Pan Lasagna

Swap out a baking dish for a smaller pan to scale down this hearty classic to serve two.

Active Time 15 minutes | **Total Time** 50 minutes

5 ounces frozen leaf spinach, thawed (3/4 cup)

5 ounces frozen broccoli florets, thawed (3/4 cup)

1 cup part-skim ricotta (8 ounces)

1 clove garlic, pressed

1/4 cup fresh basil, chopped

3 ounces part-skim mozzarella cheese, grated (about 3/4 cup)

3 tablespoons grated Pecorino Romano cheese, divided

Kosher salt

3/4 cup marinara sauce, divided

3 no-boil lasagna noodles

1. Heat the oven to 425°F. Squeeze the spinach of excess moisture and pat the broccoli as dry as possible. Chop both and place in a large bowl. Add the ricotta, garlic, and basil along with 1/2 cup mozzarella, 2 tablespoons Pecorino Romano and 1/2 teaspoon salt and stir well.

2. Spread 1/4 cup marinara in the bottom of an 8 1/2- by 4 1/2-inch loaf pan. Top with 1 noodle. Spread one-third of the remaining sauce over the top. Dollop with one-third of the ricotta mixture. Repeat. Place the remaining noodle on top, spread with the remaining sauce and dollop with the remaining ricotta mixture.

3. Sprinkle with the remaining 1/4 cup mozzarella and 1 tablespoon Pecorino Romano, cover tightly with an oiled piece of foil (to prevent sticking) and bake for 25 minutes. Uncover and bake until the noodles are tender and the top is golden brown, 10 to 12 minutes.

Serves 2
About 555 calories, 24.5 g fat (13.5 g saturated fat), 37.8 g protein, 1,585 mg sodium, 44 g carbohydrates, 6.6 g fiber

---

USE IT UP RICOTTA

JALAPEÑO POPPERS Stir together **1 cup ricotta**, **1/2 cup shredded sharp Cheddar cheese**, **1 scallion** (finely chopped) and **1/4 teaspoon kosher salt**. Spoon into **6 jalapeños** (halved lengthwise and seeded). Top with **1/2 cup finely crushed potato chips**. Bake at 375°F until chiles are tender, about 20 minutes.

Grilled Green & White Pizzas

Divvy up pizza dough into 4-ounce balls and freeze so you can thaw, top with your favorite ingredients and each enjoy your own individual pie— no sharing required! PS: Here's your excuse to fire up the grill, though you *can* cook this in a 475°F oven.

Active Time 20 minutes | **Total Time** 45 minutes

1 cup packed fresh basil leaves

2 tablespoons pine nuts

½ tablespoon fresh lemon juice

1 small clove garlic, peeled

½ cup finely grated Parmesan, divided

3 tablespoons plus 1 teaspoon olive oil, divided, plus more for brushing

Kosher salt

8 ounces summer squash, thinly sliced

8 ounces pizza dough, divided into two balls

¼ cup part-skim ricotta

1 small Fresno chile or red jalapeño, seeded and finely chopped

1. Heat the grill to medium-high and arrange the coals or set the gas burners so half will give direct heat and the other half will give indirect heat.

2. In a food processor, combine the basil, pine nuts, lemon juice, garlic, ¼ cup Parmesan, 3 tablespoons oil, ½ tablespoon water and ¼ teaspoon salt; pulse until smooth. Transfer the pesto to a medium bowl and set aside.

3. In a large bowl, toss the squash with the remaining 1 teaspoon oil and ¼ teaspoon salt until well coated. Grill until just tender, 3 to 4 minutes per side. Transfer to a bowl. Reduce the grill heat to medium.

4. Working on a floured surface, shape the pizza dough into 8-inch rounds and place on a flour-dusted baking sheet. Brush the tops with olive oil. Transfer the pizza dough to the grill over direct heat, oiled sides down, and grill, covered, until the top begins to bubble and the bottom is crisp, about 2 minutes. Use tongs to peek underneath.

5. Working quickly, brush the top of the dough with olive oil. Flip the dough to the indirect-heat side of the grill, then spread each with pesto, top with grilled zucchini and squash and dollop with ricotta. Grill, covered, until the dough is cooked through and charred on the bottom, 2 to 5 minutes more.

6. Transfer the pizzas to a large platter or cutting board and sprinkle with the remaining ¼ cup Parmesan.

Serves 2
About 700 calories, 38 g fat (8 g saturated fat), 20 g protein, 1,800 mg sodium, 68 g carbohydrates, 5 g fiber

Build the Perfect Pizza

These tasty topping combinations will put the rest of your dough to good use! Each recipe will give you two individual pies.

GRILLED PEPPERONATA PIZZA

Toss **1 small bell pepper** (seeded and cut into sixths) with **1 teaspoon olive oil**, then grill until tender and charred in spots, 8 to 10 minutes, and thinly slice. Grill the pizza dough per the master instructions at right. Flip, top the grilled pizza crusts with **marinara sauce**, **peppers** and **mozzarella** and continue grilling until the cheese melts. Sprinkle with **fresh basil** if desired.

LEMON CACIO E PEPE PIZZA

Thinly slice **1 small lemon**, brush with oil and grill until charred and tender, 1 to 2 minutes per side. In a large bowl, combine **1 1/2 ounces coarsely grated Fontina cheese**, **3/4 ounce finely grated Parmesan** and **1/4 to 1/2 teaspoon cracked black pepper**. Grill the pizza dough per the master instructions at right. Flip, then top the grilled pizza crusts with the cheese mixture, **lemon slices** and **1/2 cup fresh parsley leaves** and continue grilling per the instructions.

RICOTTA & FRESH TOMATO PIZZA

In a bowl, combine **1/2 tablespoon olive oil**, **1/2 tablespoon champagne vinegar**, **1/2 small shallot** (finely chopped), **1/2 teaspoon fresh oregano** (finely chopped), **1/4 teaspoon honey** and **a pinch each of kosher salt and pepper**. In a second bowl, mix **1/2 cup ricotta** until smooth, then stir in **2 tablespoons Pecorino Romano cheese** and a pinch each of **salt and pepper**. Grill the pizza dough per the instructions at right until fully cooked. Transfer to a cutting board and spread the cheese mixture onto the grilled pizza crusts. Slice **2 medium heirloom tomatoes** and arrange on top of the ricotta, then drizzle with the vinaigrette. Sprinkle with **basil** if desired.

How to Grill Pizza

1. Heat the grill to medium-high and arrange the coals or set the gas burners so half will give direct heat and the other half will give indirect heat.

2. Working on a floured surface, shape the pizza dough into rounds and place on a flour-dusted baking sheet. Brush the tops with olive oil.

3. Transfer the pizza dough to the grill over direct heat, oiled side down, and grill, covered, until the top begins to bubble and the bottom is crisp, about 2 minutes. Use tongs to peek underneath.

4. Working quickly, brush the top of the dough with olive oil.

5. Flip the dough to the indirect-heat side of the grill, then top as desired. Grill, covered, until the dough is cooked through and charred on the bottom, 3 to 5 minutes more (if you added cheese, it will melt).

CARAMELIZED ONIONS

Melt **1 tablespoon unsalted butter** in a medium skillet on medium-low. Add **2 small onions** (thinly sliced) to the skillet, along with **¼ teaspoon salt** and **⅛ teaspoon pepper**, and cook, covered, stirring occasionally, until tender, 8 to 10 minutes. Increase the heat to medium and cook, stirring frequently, until deep golden brown, 30 to 40 minutes. (Add 1 to 2 tablespoons water if the onions stick or the pan browns.)

Philly Cheesesteaks

Philadelphia establishments serve these subs with or without onions, topped with sliced cheese—or even Cheez Whiz. Top yours with whatever your heart desires.

Active Time 25 minutes | **Total Time** 25 minutes

2 tablespoons olive oil, divided
1 medium onion, thinly sliced
  Kosher salt and pepper
12 ounces sirloin steak, frozen for 2 hours, thinly sliced
2 ounces sliced American or provolone cheese
2 hoagie or hero rolls, warmed and split
  Sautéed mushrooms or peppers, for serving

1. Heat 1 tablespoon oil in a medium skillet on medium. Add the onion and a pinch each of salt and pepper and cook, covered, stirring occasionally, for 8 minutes. Uncover and cook, stirring until golden brown and very tender, 6 to 8 minutes more; transfer to a bowl.

3. Wipe out the skillet and heat the remaining 1 table-spoon oil on medium-high. Season the steak with ¼ teaspoon each salt and pepper and cook, tossing occasionally, until browned and cooked through, 3 to 4 minutes.

4. Lay the cheese slices over the steak, cover and cook until the cheese melts, about 2 minutes. Remove from the heat and gently fold the cheese into the steak.

5. Form sandwiches with the rolls, steak mixture and onions. Top with mushrooms or peppers if desired.

Serves 2
About 715 calories, 40 g fat (15 g saturated fat), 47 g protein, 1,445 mg sodium, 40 g carbohydrates, 3 g fiber

Ultimate Patty Melts

Grilled cheese meets burger in these epically gooey griddled sandwiches. Two sandwiches fit perfectly in a single skillet, so you won't have to worry about cooking anything in batches. (See photo on page 4.)

Active Time 15 minutes | **Total Time** 20 minutes

8 ounces ground beef chuck
  Kosher salt and pepper
3 tablespoons mayonnaise
4 thin slices rye bread
3 thin slices Swiss cheese
½ cup caramelized onions
3 thin slices American cheese

1. Shape the beef into two thin patties slightly larger than the slices of bread. Heat a large cast-iron skillet on medium-high. Season the patties with ¼ tea-spoon each salt and pepper and cook for 2 minutes per side; transfer to a plate.

2. Wipe out the skillet and return to medium-low heat. Spread the mayonnaise on 1 side of each slice of bread. Place 2 slices bread, mayonnaise sides down, in the skillet. Top each with 1 ½ slices Swiss cheese, 1 beef patty, ¼ cup caramelized onions, 1 ½ slices American cheese and the second slice of bread, mayonnaise side up. Place a small skillet (wrapped in foil) on top of the sandwiches to press and cook until the bread is golden brown and crisp, 3 minutes per side.

Serves 2
About 655 calories, 40.5 g fat (14.5 g saturated fat), 36 g protein, 1,190 mg sodium, 33 g carbohydrates, 4 g fiber

Ultimate Fried Chicken Sandwiches

What could be more comforting than crispy, juicy fried chicken? Sandwiching that chicken in soft potato rolls and piling on flavorful toppings, from hot honey and pickles to a creamy cabbage slaw.

Active Time 30 minutes | **Total Time** 35 minutes

2 small boneless, skinless chicken thighs (about 12 ounces)

½ cup low-fat buttermilk

1 teaspoon garlic powder

Kosher salt and pepper

½ cup all-purpose flour

Canola oil, for frying

2 potato rolls

Shredded romaine, sliced tomatoes, sliced pickles and hot sauce

1. In a large bowl, combine the chicken, buttermilk and garlic powder and ¼ teaspoon each salt and pepper. Place the flour in a large, shallow dish. Remove 1 piece of chicken from the buttermilk, allowing the excess to drip off; dip it in the flour, then the buttermilk, then the flour again. Place on a plate. Repeat with the remaining chicken.

2. Add 1 inch of oil to a medium skillet and heat until a deep-fry thermometer registers 325°F. Add the chicken to the skillet and fry, adjusting the heat as necessary to maintain 325°F, until the chicken is golden brown and an instant-read thermometer registers 165°F, 7 to 10 minutes per side. (If the chicken is browning too quickly, reduce the heat to medium-low for a few minutes.) Transfer to a wire rack set over a piece of foil. Sprinkle with a pinch of salt.

3. Serve on the rolls, topped with the romaine, tomato, pickles and hot sauce

Serves 2
About 720 calories, 40 g fat (5 g saturated fat), 38 g protein, 795 mg sodium, 50 g carbohydrates, 2 g fiber

---

SWITCH IT UP

A few different condiments and toppings can transform the flavors of this sandwich. These are some favorites.

honey with cayenne + sliced pickles

chipotle mayo + sliced tomato + shredded cabbage

ranch dressing + hot sauce + crumbled blue cheese + sliced red onion

pesto + provolone + chopped pepperoncini

relish + chopped sweet onion + butter lettuce

ROSEMARY-SEARED NY STRIP STEAK,
GARLICKY SAUTÉED SPINACH, AND
HASSELBACK POTATOES WITH
SCALLION BUTTER PG. 130

Chapter 5
Make It Fancy

No matter what the cause for celebration—date night, promotion, anniversary, holiday, weekend or any other special occasion—here's how to make a special "feast" that serves just two and not a crowd. Also, enjoy Mint-Pesto Baked Eggs, Raspberry "Cheesecake" French Toast and more brunch favorites at home on Saturday mornings or whenever a boring bowl of cereal just won't cut it.

Date Night Dinner

Each component of this dish is tasty on its own, but the hasselback potatoes are the true star of the plate. To make the evening extra-special, open a bottle of pinot noir, Barbera d'Alba or Syrah.
(See photo on previous page.)

Rosemary-Seared NY Strip Steak

A cast iron skillet is the secret to achieving steak-house quality at home, since it heats and cooks evenly and can handle high temperatures.

Active Time 5 minutes | **Total Time** 20 minutes

- 1 1½-inch-thick beef strip steak (about ¾ pound)
  Kosher salt and pepper
- 2 teaspoons olive oil
- 4 cloves garlic, not peeled
- 1 sprig fresh rosemary

1. Heat the oven to 425°F and a medium cast-iron skillet on medium-high. Season the steak with ½ teaspoon each salt and pepper. Add the oil to the skillet, then add the steak, garlic and rosemary. Cook until browned, about 3 minutes per side.

2. Transfer the skillet to the oven and roast until the steak is at the desired doneness, 3 to 6 minutes for medium. Transfer the steak to a cutting board and let rest for at least 5 minutes before slicing.

Serves 2
About 385 calories, 28 g fat (11 g saturated fat), 31 g protein, 555 mg sodium, 0 g carbohydrates, 0 g fiber

Garlicky Sautéed Spinach

Opt for a healthier take on the steakhouse staple and serve up wilted spinach with fragrant garlic and lemon zest, not heavy cream.

Total Time 5 minutes | **Total Time** 15 minutes

- 2 tablespoons olive oil
- 2 cloves garlic, very thinly sliced
- 1 strip lemon zest, thinly sliced
- 1 large bunch spinach, thick stems removed
  Kosher salt and pepper

1. Heat the oil, garlic and lemon zest in a large Dutch oven or skillet on medium until the garlic is beginning to turn golden around the edges, 1 to 2 minutes.

2. Add the spinach, season with ¼ teaspoon each salt and pepper and cook, tossing often, until spinach begins to wilt, 1 to 2 minutes. Remove from the heat and continue to toss until all spinach is just wilted, 1 to 2 minutes more.

Serves 2
About 165 calories, 14 g fat (2 g saturated fat), 5 g protein, 370 mg sodium, 7 g carbohydrates, 4 g fiber

Hasselback Potatoes with Scallion Butter

The accordion-like slits in these spuds are perfect for topping with savory scallion butter or anything else you want to make its way down into the crevices.

Total Time 10 minutes | **Total Time** 50 minutes

- 2 medium yellow potatoes (about 7 ounces each)
- 1 tablespoon olive oil
  Flaky sea salt and pepper
- 3 tablespoons unsalted butter, at room temperature
- 1 scallion, finely chopped

1. Heat the oven to 425°F. Cut slits in the potatoes ⅛ to ¼ inch apart, being sure to stop at least ¼ inch before the bottom (do not cut all the way through).

2. Gently toss the potatoes with the oil and ½ teaspoon each of flaky sea salt and pepper. Transfer to a small rimmed baking sheet, cut sides up. Roast until tender, golden brown and crisp, 45 to 50 minutes.

3. In a small bowl, combine the butter and scallion. Dollop the scallion butter over the potatoes.

Serves 2
About 380 calories, 24 g fat (11.5 g saturated fat), 5 g protein, 595 mg sodium, 36 g carbohydrates, 3 g fiber

TEST KITCHEN TIP

To get all these elements on the table at the same time, start with the potatoes and let them roast for 30 minutes before cooking the steak. While the steak is resting, sauté the spinach.

Pesto Linguine with Clams

Linguine con Vongole is a classic date night dish featuring noodles and fresh clams in a white wine sauce. Amp up the flavor easily with a spoonful of herby pesto.

Active Time 20 minutes | **Total Time** 20 minutes

6 ounces linguine

1 tablespoon olive oil

1 large clove garlic, thinly sliced

¼ small red chile, thinly sliced

½ cup dry white wine

Kosher salt

10 littleneck or Manila clams

½ cup plus 2 tablespoons prepared pesto

1. Cook the linguine per the package directions, then drain and return to pot.

2. Meanwhile, heat the oil in a large skillet on medium. Add garlic and chile and cook, stirring, until beginning to brown, 1 minute. Add wine and ¼ teaspoon salt and bring to a boil.

3. Add the clams, reduce the heat, and simmer, covered, just until the clams have opened, 4 to 6 minutes. Toss the clams with pesto and then linguine.

Serves 2
About 650 calories, 31.5 g fat (4.5 g saturated), 26 g protein, 900 mg sodium, 67 g carbohydrate, 4 g fiber

USE IT UP PESTO

Keep the container of pesto in the fridge to stir into scrambled eggs or soup, spread onto sandwiches or use as a marinade for chicken.

Peppercorn Pork Chops

Cooking up succulent pork chops is easy thanks to the foolproof sear, sear, roast method (see page 20). This creamy white wine pan sauce makes it restaurant-worthy fare.

Active Time 20 minutes | **Total Time** 50 minutes

1 pound Yukon gold potatoes, cut into 1-inch chunks

2 tablespoons olive oil, divided

Kosher salt and cracked black pepper

2 bone-in pork chops (1 inch thick)

1 pound green beans, trimmed

1 medium shallot, chopped

½ teaspoon fresh thyme leaves

¼ cup dry white wine

1 tablespoon mascarpone cheese

Cracked black pepper

1. Heat the oven to 425°F. Line two rimmed baking sheets with foil.

2. Toss the potatoes with ½ tablespoon oil and a pinch each of salt and cracked black pepper and spread in a single layer on one of the prepared baking sheets. Roast for 20 minutes.

3. In a medium skillet, heat 1 tablespoon oil on medium-high until very hot. Season the pork chops with ¼ teaspoon salt. Add the pork to the skillet and cook until deep golden brown, 3 minutes per side.

4. Transfer the pork to the second prepared baking sheet (don't rinse the skillet) and roast until the pork is cooked through (145°F), 10 minutes. Remove the potatoes from the oven. Toss the green beans with the remaining ½ tablespoon olive oil and spread on the baking sheet with the potatoes. Roast until the potatoes and green beans are tender and lightly browned, 10 to 15 minutes more.

5. Meanwhile, heat the skillet on medium-low. Add the shallot and thyme and cook for 2 minutes, stirring. Whisk in the wine, then the mascarpone, ½ teaspoon cracked pepper and a pinch of salt. Simmer until the sauce is reduced, 2 minutes, scraping up browned bits.

6. Serve the pork with the pan sauce, roasted potatoes and green beans.

Serves 2
About 640 calories, 31 g fat (9 g saturated fat), 36 g protein, 507 mg sodium, 59 g carbohydrates, 10.2 g fiber

Chicken & Garlic Potatoes with Red Pepper Relish

Bookmark this page just for the relish. It's fantastic served with grilled steak and seared pork or stirred into rice or orzo.

Active Time 25 minutes | **Total Time** 30 minutes

3/4 pound golden new potatoes, halved

2 1/2 tablespoons olive oil, divided

2 cloves garlic

Kosher salt and cracked black pepper

2 boneless, skinless chicken breasts

6 tablespoons roasted red peppers, chopped

3 tablespoons roasted almonds, chopped

1 scallion, finely chopped

1 1/2 tablespoons sherry vinegar

1 tablespoon chopped fresh flat-leaf parsley

1. Heat the oven to 425°F. On a rimmed baking sheet, toss the potatoes with 1 tablespoon oil and a pinch of salt. Press 1 clove of garlic over the top and toss to combine. Roast for 15 minutes.

2. Meanwhile, heat a medium skillet on medium-high. Season the chicken with a pinch each of salt and cracked pepper. Add 1 tablespoon oil to the skillet, then add the chicken and cook until browned, 4 minutes.

3. Smash the remaining clove of garlic. Flip the chicken, add the smashed garlic and cook for 1 minute. Transfer the skillet to the oven with the potatoes. Roast until the chicken is cooked through and the potatoes are golden brown and tender, 6 to 8 minutes more; transfer all to a cutting board.

4. While the chicken cooks, in a bowl, combine the red peppers, almonds, scallion and vinegar along with the remaining 1/2 tablespoon oil and a pinch of salt. Chop the smashed garlic and stir into the pepper mixture along with the parsley. Serve with the chicken and the potatoes.

Serves 2
About 515 calories, 27 g fat (3.5 g saturated fat), 32.7 g protein, 380 mg sodium, 38.4 g carbohydrates, 6.4 g fiber

Chimichurri Cauliflower "Steaks"

This dish is proof that you don't need a filet to enjoy a drizzle of chimichurri (and it gives you the perfect excuse to use up your fresh herbs).

Active Time 5 minutes | **Total Time** 20 minutes

1 large head cauliflower

1 teaspoon ground cumin

5 tablespoons canola oil

Kosher salt

¼ cup loosely packed fresh cilantro, finely chopped

¼ cup loosely packed fresh parsley, finely chopped

3 tablespoons red wine vinegar

1 small clove garlic, crushed with a press

1 jalapeño, seeded and finely chopped

1. Heat the oven to 425°F. Cut 2 slices from the center of the cauliflower (each about 1 inch thick); reserve the remaining cauliflower for another use.

2. Combine the cumin and 1 tablespoon oil and brush all over the cauliflower slices; sprinkle with ¼ teaspoon salt.

3. Heat 2 tablespoons oil in a 12-inch oven-safe skillet on medium-high until hot. Add the cauliflower and cook for 3 minutes. Turn the slices over, transfer the skillet to the oven and roast until the stems are tender, 15 to 20 minutes.

4. Meanwhile, in a small bowl, combine the cilantro, parsley, vinegar, garlic and jalapeño along with the remaining 2 tablespoons oil and ⅛ teaspoon salt. Serve the "steaks" with the herb sauce.

Serves 2

About 310 calories, 29 g fat (2 g saturated fat), 4 g protein, 505 mg sodium, 12 g carbohydrates, 5 g fiber

Seared Pork Chops with Cherries & Spinach

Cherries are in season only for a short window of time from April to August, so definitely add them to your shopping cart—and your dinner rotation!—the second they start to hit the produce section.

Active Time 15 minutes | **Total Time** 30 minutes

1 tablespoon olive oil

2 6-ounce boneless pork chops

   Kosher salt and pepper

½ cup cherries, pitted
   and halved

2 tablespoons dry white wine

1 teaspoon whole-grain mustard

1 bunch spinach, thick
   stems discarded

1. Heat the oil in a large skillet on medium. Pat the pork chops dry with paper towels and season with ¼ teaspoon each salt and pepper. Cook until golden brown and just cooked through, 8 to 10 minutes per side; transfer to plates.

2. Add the cherries to the skillet and cook, stirring occasionally, until beginning to soften, about 2 minutes. Add the wine and cook until reduced to ½ tablespoon, about 2 minutes more.

3. Stir in the mustard and 2 tablespoons water, then the spinach, and cook, tossing, until the spinach begins to wilt, about 2 minutes. Serve with the pork.

Serves 2
About 475 calories, 31 g fat (9 g saturated fat), 37.8 g protein, 445 mg sodium, 11.7 g carbohydrates, 3.7 g fiber

---

TEST KITCHEN TIP

No cherry pitter? Use a chopstick to push out the pit, or smash ripe cherries with your hand and then use a spoon.

Anchovy Brown Butter Linguine with Parmesan Breadcrumbs

Consider a humble box of noodles your blank canvas for the most delicious last-minute dinner, with a little help from pantry staples. Freshly toasted breadcrumbs, nutty brown butter, salty anchovies and Parmesan cheese elevate this simple pasta dish.

Active Time 20 minutes | **Total Time** 20 minutes

6 ounces linguine

1 ½ ounces fresh sourdough bread (without crust), torn

½ ounce Parmesan, grated

½ tablespoon olive oil

Kosher salt

1 tablespoon fresh flat-leaf parsley, chopped

½ tablespoon grated lemon zest

2 tablespoons unsalted butter

2 small anchovy fillets, chopped

½ medium shallot, finely chopped

1. Heat the oven to 400°F. Cook the pasta according to the package directions. Reserve ¼ cup of the cooking water, then drain the pasta.

2. In a food processor, pulse the bread, Parmesan and oil and ⅛ teaspoon salt to form fine crumbs. Transfer to a rimmed baking sheet and bake, tossing once, until golden brown, 6 to 8 minutes. Toss with the parsley and lemon zest.

3. Meanwhile, melt the butter in a medium skillet on medium-high. When the butter is melted, continue to simmer, whisking constantly, until deep brown flecks appear, 2 to 5 minutes.

4. Reduce the heat to low, add the anchovies and shallot and cook until the shallot is tender, 1 to 2 minutes. Toss with the pasta and 2 tablespoons of the reserved pasta cooking water, adding more water if the pasta seems dry. Serve topped with the Parmesan crumbs.

Serves 2
About 540 calories, 19 g fat (9.5 g saturated fat), 17 g protein, 585 mg sodium, 77 g carbohydrates, 4 g fiber

TEST KITCHEN TIP
Pair this pasta with something fizzy, like a glass of Cava or a dry Prosecco.

White Wine Mussels

Making mussels at home isn't as intimidating as you may think. Start with this basic white wine sauce, then get creative with different flavors.

Active Time 20 minutes | **Total Time** 20 minutes

2 pounds mussels

1 tablespoon olive oil

2 cloves garlic, finely chopped

1/8 teaspoon red pepper flakes

1 cup dry white wine

Kosher salt

1 1/2 tablespoons cold unsalted butter

2 tablespoons fresh flat-leaf parsley, roughly chopped

Crusty bread and lemon wedges, for serving (optional)

1. Scrub the mussels under cold water, then remove the furry threads (called the beard) by grabbing them between your thumb and forefinger and pulling down toward the hinged end of the shell. (A paper towel can help you grip them.)

2. Heat the oil, garlic and red pepper flakes in a large Dutch oven on medium-low until the garlic is beginning to turn golden brown, 4 minutes. Add the wine and bring to a boil; boil for 2 minutes.

3. Add 1/8 teaspoon salt, then the mussels, and cook, covered, stirring once or twice, until the shells open, about 6 minutes (discard any mussels whose shells do not open).

4. Add the butter and cook, stirring, for 2 minutes. Toss with the parsley and serve with bread and lemon wedges if desired.

Serves 2
About 280 calories, 18.5 g fat (7 g saturated fat), 17 g protein, 515 mg sodium, 10 g carbohydrates, 0 g fiber

---

SWITCH IT UP

Sauté seeds, veggies or meat with garlic in the base recipe, then stir in the remaining ingredients along with the wine.

CREAMY TARRAGON 2 teaspoons Dijon mustard + 1/4 cup heavy cream + 1 tablespoon tarragon

SPICED TOMATO 1 teaspoon fennel seeds + 8 ounces chopped heirloom tomatoes + 2 tablespoons chopped fresh basil

SMOKY ORANGE 1 1/2 ounces diced Spanish chorizo + 1/4 cup halved pitted green olives + 1 tablespoon grated orange zest

Roasted Cumin Shrimp and Asparagus

This low-cook dinner is perfect for a night when you're feeling a little lazy, yet you still want a meal worthy of an accompanying glass of wine.

Active Time 20 minutes | **Total Time** 45 minutes

½ cup couscous

½ orange, divided

   Kosher salt and pepper

8 ounces asparagus

½ tablespoon olive oil

10 large peeled and deveined shrimp

¼ teaspoon ground cumin

⅛ teaspoon cayenne

1. Bring ¾ cup water to a boil. Place the couscous in a bowl. Top with the juice of ¼ orange and then ½ cup hot water. Cover and let sit for 10 minutes, then fluff and season with salt and pepper.

2. Meanwhile, heat the broiler. On a rimmed baking sheet, toss the asparagus with the oil, then season with salt and pepper to taste. Broil for 3 minutes.

3. Season the shrimp with the cumins and cayenne and ⅛ teaspoon salt and arrange on the sheet with the asparagus. Broil until the shrimp are just opaque throughout and the asparagus is just tender, 3 to 4 minutes more.

4. Squeeze the remaining ¼ orange over the shrimp and asparagus and serve with the couscous.

Serves 2
About 270 calories, 7.5 g fat (1 g saturated fat), 12 g protein, 445 mg sodium, 39 g carbohydrates, 4 g fiber

PICKLED ASPARAGUS STEMS

Trim ¼ inch from the ends of **asparagus stems**. Place the stems in a 16-ounce canning jar along with **1 clove garlic** (sliced), **½ teaspoon whole coriander seeds**, **¼ teaspoon black peppercorns** and **⅛ teaspoon red pepper flakes**. In a small saucepan, combine **½ cup water**, **⅓ cup distilled white vinegar**, **½ tablespoon sugar** and **1 teaspoon kosher salt** and bring to a boil. Reduce the heat and simmer until the sugar and salt have dissolved, about 3 minutes. Remove from the heat. Cool for 5 minutes, then pour over the asparagus to cover. Let cool to room temperature. Refrigerate for at least 2 days and up to 2 weeks.

Grilled Salmon Niçoise

Bring the party outside with this sophisticated salmon medley that's cooked primarily on the grill.

Active Time 20 minutes | **Total Time** 20 minutes

1 tablespoon red wine vinegar

½ teaspoon Dijon mustard

1½ tablespoons olive oil, divided
   Kosher salt and pepper

2 tablespoons pitted Kalamata olives, finely chopped

½ tablespoon capers, rinsed

2 tablespoons fresh tarragon, chopped

8 ounces fingerling potatoes, halved lengthwise

4 ounces green beans

1 12-ounce center-cut salmon fillet (skin on), about 1 inch thick

½ head butter lettuce, leaves separated

2 large hard-boiled eggs, quartered

1. Heat a grill to medium-high.

2. In a medium bowl, whisk together the vinegar, the mustard, 1 tablespoon oil and ⅛ teaspoon pepper. Add the olives, capers and tarragon and mix to combine.

3. In a separate medium bowl, toss the potatoes and green beans with the remaining ½ tablespoon oil and ⅛ teaspoon each salt and pepper. Season the salmon with ⅛ teaspoon each salt and pepper and grill, skin side down, covered, until opaque throughout, 10 to 12 minutes; transfer to a cutting board.

4. While the salmon is grilling, add the potatoes to the grill and cook, covered, until tender, 5 to 6 minutes per side, then add to the bowl with the dressing and toss. Grill the green beans until lightly charred, turning occasionally, 2 to 3 minutes.

5. Using a fork, flake the salmon into pieces, discarding the skin. Divide the lettuce, eggs, potatoes, green beans and salmon between two plates, spooning any remaining dressing over the top.

Serves 2

About 570 calories, 34 g fat (6 g saturated fat), 39 g protein, 600 mg sodium, 27 g carbohydrates, 5 g fiber

TEST KITCHEN TIP

If the salmon skin sticks to the grill, simply slide a spatula between the skin and the fish and lift off the fillet. Once the grill is cool, you can scrape the skin from it.

Lemon-Thyme Butterflied Roast Chicken

Decades ago, a recipe for roast chicken made its way through the staff of *Glamour* magazine, and as the editors cooked it for their partners, they became engaged shortly afterward. The dish was lovingly dubbed "Engagement Chicken" and has been credited with dozens of marriage proposals since—or so the story goes. *This* version may not guarantee an engagement, but it's still delicious, and because you're removing the backbone (a.k.a. butterflying), it spends much less time in the oven.

Active Time 20 minutes | **Total Time** 45 minutes

2 heads garlic, halved through the equators

2 lemons, 1 sliced and 1 cut into wedges

2 tablespoons olive oil, divided

½ bunch fresh thyme, divided

1 3 ½- to 4-pound chicken, backbone removed

Kosher salt and pepper

1. Heat oven to 425°F. On a large rimmed baking sheet, toss the garlic halves and sliced lemon with 1 tablespoon oil and half the thyme; arrange in the center of the sheet. Place the chicken on top, rub with the remaining 1 tablespoon oil and season with ½ teaspoon each salt and pepper. Scatter the lemon wedges around it and roast for 20 minutes.

2. Scatter the remaining thyme around the chicken and roast until the chicken is golden brown and cooked through (165°F on an instant-read thermometer inserted into the thickest part of the thigh), about 30 minutes more.

Serves 2
About 475 calories, 27 g fat (7 g saturated fat), 49 g protein, 385 mg sodium, 6 g carbohydrates, 1 g fiber

---

HOW TO BUTTERFLY A CHICKEN

Remove the neck and giblets and pat the chicken dry. Using kitchen shears, cut along one side of the backbone, then cut the other side. Flip the chicken over so the inside is facing up. Using a heavy knife, notch each side of the breastbone to help flatten it. Turn the chicken back over. Hold the chicken by each breast, pull up and, with your thumbs, push the breastbone downward. Use the ball of your hand and break the breastbone. Tuck the wing tips behind the breasts to prevent burning while roasting.

Chicken Roulade with Marinated Tomatoes

Chicken breasts are transformed into a dinner party-worthy dish with the addition of spinach and Parmesan. Rolling the chicken makes for a pretty presentation. Plus, it means you'll get a taste of the cheesy, garlicky spinach filling with every bite.

Active Time 35 minutes | **Total Time** 35 minutes

2 boneless, skinless
  chicken breasts

1 clove garlic, grated

1 tablespoon grated lemon zest
  plus 1 tablespoon lemon juice

¼ cup finely grated Parmesan

16 baby spinach leaves
  Kosher salt and pepper

2 tablespoons olive oil, divided

1 pint grape or cherry
  tomatoes, sliced

⅛ small red onion, thinly sliced

1 tablespoon red wine vinegar

1. Heat the oven to 450°F. Pound the chicken breasts into thin cutlets. In a small bowl, combine the garlic, lemon zest and Parmesan. Lay 8 spinach leaves on each chicken cutlet, then sprinkle the garlic mixture on top. Roll the chicken up and secure with a toothpick (place the toothpick parallel to the seam to make turning the roulades easier). Season the chicken with ¼ teaspoon each salt and pepper.

2. Heat 1 tablespoon oil in a medium ovenproof skillet on medium-high. Carefully add the roulades, seam sides down, and cook, turning, until browned on all sides, 6 to 7 minutes. Transfer to the oven and bake until cooked through, 8 to 9 minutes more. Drizzle the lemon juice on the roulades.

3. While the chicken roasts, toss together the tomatoes, onion and vinegar, the remaining 1 tablespoon oil and ¼ teaspoon each salt and pepper. Serve with the chicken.

Serves 2
About 345 calories, 19.5 g fat (4 g saturated fat), 32 g protein, 760 mg sodium, 17.9 g carbohydrates, 2.7 g fiber

Savory Lentil Waffles

Here is proof you should pull out the waffle iron for more than just a stack of buttermilk Belgian waffles. This can work as breakfast-for-dinner, brunch, lunch, you name it.

Active Time 20 minutes **| Total Time** 20 minutes

1 cup cooked and drained lentils, rinsed

⅛ small red onion, thinly sliced

2 tablespoons golden raisins, chopped

1½ tablespoons olive oil

1½ tablespoons sherry vinegar

½ cup store-bought dry waffle mix, plus other batter ingredients specified in package directions

½ teaspoon curry powder

⅛ teaspoon ground coriander

Kosher salt and pepper

2 cups baby arugula

2 tablespoons toasted almonds, chopped

Greek yogurt, for serving

1. In a small bowl, combine the lentils, onion, raisins, oil and vinegar.

2. In a medium bowl, whisk together the waffle mix, curry powder and coriander and a pinch each of salt and pepper. Stir in the additional ingredients as directed on the waffle mix package. Prepare 1 waffle in a preheated waffle maker per manufacturer's directions.

3. When the waffle is cooked, toss the arugula and almonds with the lentil mixture. Split the waffle and spread with yogurt if desired. Top with the lentil salad.

Serves 2
About 390 calories, 16 g fat (2 g saturated fat), 13 g protein, 505 mg sodium, 50 g carbohydrates, 10 g fiber

---

CAPRESE WAFFLES

Prepare batter with **½ cup dry waffle mix** according to the package directions; fold in **2 tablespoons grated Pecorino Romano cheese** and prepare 1 waffle in a waffle maker. In a bowl, whisk together **1 tablespoon olive oil** with **½ tablespoon red wine vinegar** and **⅛ teaspoon each kosher salt and pepper**. Stir in **½ small shallot** (finely chopped). Toss with **8 ounces mixed-color cherry tomatoes** (halved), **2 ounces salami** (cut into small cubes) and **2 tablespoons fresh basil** (torn); fold in **4 ounces fresh mozzarella** (torn). Split the waffle and spoon the salad on top.

FROM LEFT
AVOCADO DIP, PG. 188
VEGAN QUESO, PG. 194
BUFFALO CHICKEN DIP, PG. 192
FRENCH ONION DIP, PG. 190

Chapter 6

Happy Hour

Bring the party home—sans the, well, party—with these perfectly portioned cocktails, apps and snacks, organized into easy-to-pull-off menus.

Staycation Sips & Dips

Whip up a spread of signature drinks and flavor-forward dips inspired by the places you love to travel so you can enjoy a mini "vacation" at a moment's notice. Pick one cocktail to enjoy or try them all! Choose your own adventure.

Pimm's Cup

Popular in Great Britain, this refreshing drink is packed with fresh herbs and fruit.

Active Time 5 minutes
Total Time 5 minutes

- 4 ounces Pimm's No. 1
- 1 mini cucumber, sliced
- 2 strawberries, sliced
- 1 lemon, sliced
- 1 bunch fresh mint
  Ice
- 6 ounces Limonata or sparkling lemonade

In a measuring cup, stir together the Pimm's No. 1, cucumber, strawberry and lemon slices and a few fresh mint leaves along with ice. Divide between two glasses. Top each glass with 3 ounces Limonata.

Serves 2
About 135 calories, 0 g fat (0 g saturated fat), 0.8 g protein, 5 mg sodium, 13 g carbohydrates, 1.2 g fiber

Caipirinha

Cachaça, a Brazilian spirit distilled from fermented sugarcane juice, is the base of this simple cocktail.

Active Time 5 minutes
Total Time 5 minutes

- 1 lime, cut into wedges, plus more for serving
- 4 teaspoons sugar
- 4 ounces cachaça
- Crushed ice, for serving

In a cocktail shaker, muddle the lime wedges with the sugar to squeeze out the lime juice. Add the cachaça and shake, then strain into two glasses filled with crushed ice. Serve with additional lime wedges.

Serves 2
About 170 calories, 0 g fat (0 g saturated fat), 0 g protein, 0 mg sodium, 12 g carbohydrates, 1 g fiber

Pisco Sour

This frothy, tart Peruvian drink is fizzy from forceful shaking and the addition of egg whites.

Active Time 5 minutes
Total Time 5 minutes

- Ice
- 5 ounces pisco
- 1 ounce fresh lime juice
- 1 ounce fresh lemon juice
- 1 ounce simple syrup
- 2 egg whites
- Angostura bitters, for topping

To a cocktail shaker with ice, add the pisco, lime juice, lemon juice, simple syrup and egg whites. Shake vigorously, then strain into two glasses and top each drink with a couple of drops of bitters.

Serves 2
About 285 calories, 0 g fat (0 g saturated fat), 3.7 g protein, 55 mg sodium, 22.4 g carbohydrates, 0.1 g fiber

Dark and Stormy

One sip of this drink can transport you to Bermuda. Rum hovers like stormy clouds over ginger beer.

Active Time 5 minutes
Total Time 5 minutes

- Ice
- 1 ounce fresh lime juice
- 6 ounces ginger beer
- 4 ounces dark rum
- Candied ginger, for serving

Fill two glasses with ice. To each glass, add ½ ounce lime juice and 3 ounces ginger beer; then top with 2 ounces dark rum. Garnish with candied ginger.

Serves 2
About 190 calories, 0 g fat (0 g saturated fat), 0.1 g protein, 5 mg sodium, 15.5 g carbohydrates, 0.1 g fiber

TEST KITCHEN TIP

In a pinch, you can sub rum for the cachaça.

Spinach & Yogurt Dip

Frozen spinach is prechopped and blanched, making it the ultimate shortcut ingredient. Devote the time to thawing and squeezing the excess moisture out of the spinach; otherwise the dip will be watery.

Active Time 20 minutes | **Total Time** 20 minutes

1½ tablespoons olive oil, divided

¼ small onion, finely chopped

½ small clove garlic, finely chopped

2 ounces frozen leaf spinach, thawed and squeezed dry

½ cup plain Greek yogurt

1 teaspoon fresh lemon juice

Kosher salt and pepper

1 tablespoon fresh mint leaves, chopped

Assorted flatbreads, for serving

1. Heat 1 tablespoon oil on medium in a medium skillet. Cook the onion, stirring occasionally, until tender, 3 to 5 minutes. Stir in the garlic and cook for 2 minutes; transfer to a bowl.

2. Chop the spinach and toss with the onion mixture. Fold in the yogurt, the lemon juice and ⅛ teaspoon each salt and pepper.

3. Heat the remaining ½ tablespoon oil in the skillet until shimmering. Add the mint and cook until sizzling and fragrant, about 1 minute. Let cool slightly, then spoon over the yogurt dip. Serve with assorted flatbreads.

Serves 2
About 165 calories, 13.5 g fat (3 g saturated fat), 7 g protein, 165 mg sodium, 5.3 g carbohydrates, 1.2 g fiber

---

USE IT UP FROZEN SPINACH

Use some of the remaining package of frozen spinach in Loaf Pan Lasagna (page 118).

Roasted Red Pepper Dip

Muhammara is a spicy Syrian dip traditionally made with Aleppo peppers, but those can sometimes be difficult to find. This version uses charred roasted red peppers and cayenne to get close to that signature flavor.

Active Time 10 minutes | **Total Time** 35 minutes | **Makes** 1 1/3 cups

1 medium red pepper,
halved and seeded

1 tablespoon olive oil, divided,
plus more for serving

1/4 tablespoons walnuts,
plus more for serving

1 1/2 teaspoons fresh lemon juice

1 small clove garlic,
finely chopped

1/4 teaspoon ground sumac

1/8 teaspoon cayenne

Kosher salt

2 tablespoons fresh
breadcrumbs

Pomegranate molasses,
for serving (optional)

Assorted flatbreads,
for serving

1. Rub the pepper halves with 1/2 tablespoon oil and place, cut sides down, on a foil-lined baking sheet. Broil until the skin starts to blacken, 8 to 10 minutes. Immediately transfer to a bowl, cover with plastic wrap and let sit until tender, 12 minutes. Remove the skins and discard.

2. In a food processor, pulse the pepper, walnuts, lemon juice, garlic, sumac, cayenne and the remaining 1/2 tablespoon oil along with 1/4 teaspoon salt until mostly smooth but still a bit chunky. Stir in the breadcrumbs.

3. Transfer to a serving bowl. Drizzle with olive oil and pomegranate molasses if desired and sprinkle with additional walnuts. Serve with assorted flatbreads.

Per Serving (5 tablespoons)
About 40 calories, 3 g fat (0.5 g saturated fat), 0.6 g protein, 125 mg sodium, 3.3 g carbohydrates, 0.3 g fiber

TEST KITCHEN TIP

Aleppo peppers can be found at Middle Eastern grocery stores or purchased online.

Yellow Split Pea Dip

Enjoy a taste of Greece without having to set up the whole mezze platter: Choose just one element, scale it down, pick up some pita bread and you have an appetizer for two!

Active Time 10 minutes **| Total Time** 1 hour 10 minutes **| Makes** 1 ¼ cups

½ cup yellow split peas

½ small yellow onion, finely chopped

1 small clove garlic, pressed

½ small bay leaf

¼ teaspoon ground turmeric

Kosher salt

1 tablespoon olive oil, plus more for serving

1 ½ teaspoons fresh lemon juice

Finely chopped red onion, finely chopped fresh parsley and paprika, for serving

Assorted flatbreads, for serving

1. In a small saucepan, combine the split peas with 1 ¼ cup water and bring to a boil, skimming the foam that rises to the surface. Lower the heat and add the yellow onion, garlic, bay leaf and turmeric and ¼ teaspoon salt and simmer until the split peas are very tender, 50 to 60 minutes.

2. Discard the bay leaf and transfer to a food processor with any remaining liquid. Add the oil and lemon juice and puree until smooth.

3. Transfer to a serving bowl, drizzle with additional oil and top with the red onion, parsley and a sprinkle of paprika if desired. Serve with assorted flatbreads.

Per Serving (5 tablespoons)
About 130 calories, 4.5 g fat (0.5 g saturated fat), 6 g protein, 120 mg sodium, 18 g carbohydrates, 7 g fiber

TEST KITCHEN TIP

Have leftovers? This dip will keep in the fridge up to 1 week. Serve leftovers with crudités or spread on a sandwich!

Tequila & Tortillas

Consider this the scaled-down (homemade!) version of a night spent at your local Mexican restaurant enjoying pitchers of margaritas and diving headfirst into a never-ending basket of chips and salsa.

Classic Margarita

A pitcher of this popular cocktail will bring the party to wherever you are! This recipe makes only two drinks, though you can definitely double or triple it if desired.

Active Time 5 minutes
Total Time 5 minutes

- 6 **tablespoons tequila**
- ¼ **cup fresh lime juice, plus lime slices for serving**
- ¼ **cup Cointreau**
  Coarse salt, for serving
  Finely grated lime zest, for serving

1. In a small pitcher, combine the tequila, lime juice and Cointreau. If desired, rub the rims of two glasses with a lime slice and dip in salt and lime zest to coat.

2. Add ice to each glass and pour the margarita over it. Serve with lime slices.

Serves 2
About 185 calories, 0 g fat (0 g saturated fat), 0.1 g protein, 0 mg sodium, 13.1 g carbohydrates, 0.3 g fiber

Jalapeño Mango-rita

The secret to a killer margarita? Sourcing the best ingredients you can find, including premium white tequila and the freshest limes. Then dial it up a notch by adding a balance of heat and sweetness—fiery jalapeño and chili powder plus agave nectar and mango juice.

Active Time 5 minutes
Total Time 5 minutes

- ½ tablespoon chili powder
- 1 teaspoon sugar
  Kosher salt
- 1 cup mango juice
- ¾ cup tequila
- ¼ cup fresh lime juice
- 2 tablespoons agave nectar or honey
- ½ jalapeño, cut in half
  Lime wedges, for serving

1. On a plate, combine the chili powder, the sugar and ½ tablespoon salt.

2. In a small pitcher, combine the mango juice, tequila, lime juice, agave nectar and jalapeño. Refrigerate until slightly spicy, 1 to 3 hours. Discard the jalapeño.

3. When ready to serve, run a lime wedge along the rims of 2 glasses and dip in the sugar mixture to coat. Add ice to each glass and pour the margarita mixture over it. Serve with lime wedges.

Serves 2
About 370 calories, 0 g fat (0 g saturated fat), 0.7 g protein, 770 mg sodium, 45.3 g carbohydrates, 2.1 g fiber

Grapefruit-Ginger Paloma

Margaritas may get all the attention, but the paloma deserves praise too. In lieu of Cointreau, it gets its fresh citrus flavor from grapefruit and a squeeze of lime, resulting in a slightly less sweet—yet still refreshing—tequila drink.

Active Time 5 minutes
Total Time 5 minutes

- ⅓ cup fresh red grapefruit juice
- 4 teaspoons fresh lime juice
- ¾ teaspoon sugar
- ⅓ cup tequila
- ⅓ cup ginger beer

In a pitcher, combine the grapefruit juice, lime juice and sugar and stir to dissolve; add the tequila. Pour into two glasses over ice and top with ginger beer.

Serves 2
About 130 calories, 0 g fat (0 g saturated fat), 0.2 g protein, 0 mg sodium, 11.5 g carbohydrates, 0.1 g fiber

Fresh Salsa

Many store-bought salsas are delicious, but whipping up a batch from scratch results in a dip that tastes fresher and more flavorful. Plus, this recipe yields less than 2 cups, so you'll have plenty for dunking tortilla chips but not so much that you'll be stuck brainstorming ways to work your way through a half-eaten jar.

Active Time 10 minutes | **Total Time** 10 minutes
Makes 1 3/4 cups

  1 jalapeño (seeded, if desired), finely chopped
  1/4 small white onion, finely chopped
  1 tablespoon fresh lime juice
      Kosher salt and pepper
  8 ounces plum tomatoes, halved, seeded and chopped
  1/4 cup fresh cilantro leaves, chopped
      Tortilla chips, for serving

1. In a large bowl, toss the jalapeño and onion with the lime juice, 1/4 teaspoon salt and 1/4 teaspoon pepper; let sit for 10 minutes.

2. Toss with the tomatoes, then fold in the cilantro. Serve with tortilla chips.

Per Serving (1/2 cup)
About 15 calories, 0 g fat (0 g saturated fat), 1 g protein, 140 mg sodium, 4 g carbohydrates, 1 g fiber

Chunky Guacamole

Grab a bag of tortilla chips and get ready to scoop up this five-ingredient dip studded with pieces of avocado, jalapeño, cilantro and onions. If you're not a fan of raw onions, try soaking them in water for a few minutes to mellow the flavor before draining them and tossing them into the bowl.

Active Time 10 minutes | **Total Time** 10 minutes
Makes 1 1/2 cups

  2 small ripe avocados, diced
  1/8 small white onion, finely chopped
  2 tablespoons cilantro, chopped
  1/2 jalapeño, seeded and finely chopped
  1 tablespoon fresh lime juice
      Kosher salt

In a medium bowl, gently combine all the ingredients with 1/2 teaspoon salt.

Per Serving (1/2 cup)
About 165 calories, 15 g fat (2 g saturated fat), 2 g protein, 330 mg sodium, 10 g carbohydrates, 7 g fiber

At-Home Speakeasy

No need to memorize a password or find a secret entrance to get into *this* party. Simply shake up a Prohibition-inspired cocktail and serve it with an assortment of sophisticated bites.

The Bee's Sneeze

A dash of black pepper—as well as a homemade honey-pepper syrup—gives the classic Bee's Knees cocktail some extra sass.

Active Time 10 minutes | **Total Time** 10 minutes plus cooling

½ cup honey

½ teaspoon cracked black pepper

4 ounces gin

2 ounces fresh lemon juice

Cracked black pepper, for serving

1. In a saucepan, simmer the honey, 3 tablespoons water and the pepper until the honey dissolves. Let cool, then strain. Makes a generous ½ cup. Store syrup in a cool, dry place up to 1 month.

2. Fill a cocktail shaker with ice and add the gin, lemon juice and 2 tablespoons of the syrup. Shake vigorously, then strain into two coupes and sprinkle with the pepper if desired.

Serves 2
About 200 calories, 0 g fat (0 g saturated fat), 0.2 g protein, 0 mg sodium, 19.4 g carbohydrates, 0.1 g fiber

---

USE IT UP HONEY-PEPPER SYRUP

Make a vinaigrette: Whisk together **1 tablespoon lemon juice**, **2 teaspoons each honey-pepper syrup and Dijon mustard** and **¼ teaspoon salt** to combine. Then whisk in **2 to 3 tablespoons olive oil** and toss with your favorite **mixed greens**.

Wild Mushroom Toasts

A medley of mushrooms transforms a piece of bread into a beautiful hors d'oeuvre. Try a mix of flavorful varieties such as creminis, shiitakes, oyster mushrooms and King Trumpets.

Active Time 25 minutes | **Total Time** 25 minutes

1 tablespoon olive oil, or more if needed

8 ounces mixed mushrooms, sliced or quartered

Kosher salt and pepper

½ red chile, thinly sliced

2 tablespoons fresh flat-leaf parsley, chopped

¼ cup fresh ricotta

¼ cup goat cheese, softened

2 thick slices country bread, toasted

1. Heat a large skillet on medium-high. Add the oil and mushrooms (taking care not to overcrowd the pan) and cook, tossing occasionally, until golden brown and tender, 4 to 6 minutes. Season with salt and pepper, transfer to a bowl and repeat with any remaining mushrooms if necessary, adding more oil if needed.

2. Add the chile to the skillet and sauté until tender; mix with the mushrooms and parsley.

3. In a bowl, combine the ricotta and goat cheese. Spread on the toasts, then top with the mushroom mixture.

Serves 2

About 475 calories, 16.5 g fat (6 g saturated fat), 20 g protein, 800 mg sodium, 63 g carbohydrates, 6 g fiber

Cherry Tomato Confit

Toss tomatoes with herbs, oil and garlic, roast them until they burst and keep the confit in the fridge to pile on top of baguette slices schmeared with ricotta for the easiest appetizer ever. (See photo on page 17.)

Active Time 15 minutes | **Total Time** 1 hour
Makes 2 cups

2 pints cherry tomatoes

3 cloves garlic, smashed and peeled

3 sprigs fresh thyme

2 tablespoons olive oil, plus more for storing

Kosher salt and pepper

Toasted baguette slices and ricotta, for serving

1. Heat the oven to 350°F. On a small rimmed baking sheet, toss the tomatoes with the garlic, thyme and oil and ⅛ teaspoon each salt and pepper. Bake until the tomatoes are wrinkled and fragrant, 30 to 40 minutes, shaking the pan halfway through. Let cool.

2. Use the confit on bruschetta: Spread ricotta onto toasted baguette slices, then top with the confit. To store, transfer to a jar, top with oil and refrigerate for up to 1 week.

Per Serving (¼ cup)
About 45 calories, 4 g fat (1 g saturated fat), 1 g protein, 35 mg sodium, 3 g carbohydrates, 1 g fiber

---

CAPRESE BITES

No time to roast? Slide **grape tomatoes** onto toothpicks or small skewers with **bocconcini** and **basil**. Drizzle with balsamic vinegar and serve.

Frico Salad Bites

Salad makes a fun drinking companion when served in a cheesy poppable cup. Try one of these three salad combinations.

FRICO CUPS

Active Time 10 minutes | **Total Time** 15 minutes plus cooling | **Makes** 8

1½ cups grated Parmesan

1. Heat oven to 375°F. Line a baking sheet with parchment paper. Make 8 piles of Parmesan (3 tablespoons each) on the prepared baking sheet, spacing 2 inches apart. Bake until melted but not quite brown, 6 minutes.

2. Use a thin metal spatula to quickly transfer the cheese to a muffin pan, pressing lightly in the centers. Cool before filling.

GRAPE TOMATO, OLIVE & FETA

Active Time 10 minutes
Total Time 20 minutes plus cooling

- 2 cups grape tomatoes, halved
- 2 tablespoons sliced pitted green olives
- 3 tablespoons crumbled feta cheese
- ½ tablespoon sherry vinegar
- ½ tablespoon olive oil
  Kosher salt and pepper
  Fresh basil, for serving
  Frico Cups (see left)

While the Frico Cups cool, in a medium bowl, combine the tomatoes, olives, feta, vinegar and oil. Season to taste with salt and pepper. Divide the salad among the Frico Cups and garnish with basil.

Serves 2 (4 salad bites)
*About 360 calories,
24.5 g fat (12 g saturated fat),
12.2 g protein, 1,365 mg sodium,
23.3 g carbohydrates, 2.3 g fiber*

SESAME, RADISH & CUCUMBER

Active Time 10 minutes
Total Time 20 minutes plus cooling

- ½ English cucumber, chopped
- 2 small radishes, sliced
- ½ tablespoon fresh lime juice
- 1 teaspoon toasted sesame oil
- 1 tablespoon black and white sesame seeds
  Kosher salt and pepper
  Frico Cups (see left)

While the Frico Cups cool, toss the cucumber and radishes with the lime juice, sesame oil and sesame seeds. Season to taste with salt and pepper. Divide among the Frico Cups.

Serves 2 (4 salad bites)
*About 305 calories,
21 g fat (10 g saturated fat),
18.7 g protein, 1,140 mg sodium,
12.1 g carbohydrates, 1.4 g fiber*

FARRO, CORN & SCALLION

Active Time 10 minutes
Total Time 20 minutes plus cooling

- 2 ears corn, husked
- 1 cup cooked farro
- 1 scallion, thinly sliced
- 1½ tablespoons fresh lemon juice
- 1 tablespoon olive oil
  Kosher salt and pepper
  Frico Cups (see left)

While the Frico Cups cool, grill the corn for 10 minutes, turning occasionally. Remove from the grill and let cool. Cut the kernels off into a large bowl, then toss with the farro, scallion, lemon juice and oil. Season to taste with salt and pepper. Divide among the Frico Cups.

Serves 2 (4 salad bites)
*About 505 calories,
25.5 g fat (10.5 g saturated fat),
24.5 g protein, 1,155 mg sodium,
48 g carbohydrates, 4.9 g fiber*

Make It A Mocktail

Every bit as festive as its boozier counterpart, this classic mocktail will have you feeling like a kid again. Pair it with grown-up appetizers—including a cheesy "campfire" dip and garlicky bruschetta toasts—to balance it all out.

Gingery Shirley Temple

This drink was reportedly created for the famous child actress in the 1930s after she complained that she wanted to drink like the grown-ups. It turned out that Shirley (at least once she was an adult) thought the drink was too sweet. Enter this toned-down version of the nonalcoholic favorite.

Active Time 10 minutes | **Total Time** 35 minutes
Serves 2, plus additional syrup

3/4 cup sugar

3/4 cup pomegranate juice

1 1/2-inch piece fresh ginger, peeled and thinly sliced

Club soda

2 maraschino cherries

2 slices candied ginger

1. In a small saucepan, combine the sugar, pomegranate juice and fresh ginger and simmer, stirring once halfway through, until the sugar dissolves, about 12 minutes. Remove from the heat and let cool to room temperature (about 15 minutes); strain. Makes 1 cup. Store syrup in an airtight container in the fridge for up to 1 week.

2. Fill two Collins glasses with ice. Add 1 tablespoon of the pomegranate-ginger syrup to each glass and top with club soda. Serve with the cherries and candied ginger.

Serves 2
About 70 calories, 0 g fat (0 g saturated fat), 0 g protein, 45 mg sodium, 17.6 g carbohydrates, 0.2 g fiber

---

FIZZY FRUITY FLOATS

Add **1 scoop lime sorbet** to each glass and pour **coconut-flavored sparkling water** over the top. (Mix up the flavors and try mango sorbet and lime-flavored sparkling water or blood orange sorbet and plain sparkling water.) Add straws and serve.

Garlicky Roasted-Radish Bruschetta

Radishes have a bad rap for tasting bitter, but a stint in the oven helps mellow out their flavor a bit. Toss them with herbs, then spoon over toasts for a fresh appetizer.

Active Time 10 minutes | **Total Time** 25 minutes

1 ½ tablespoons olive oil, divided
12 ounces small to medium radishes, mixed colors, trimmed and halved (quartered if large), leaves reserved
2 cloves garlic, 1 thinly sliced
2 slices country bread
1 tablespoon chopped fresh flat-leaf parsley
Kosher salt and pepper

1. Heat the oven to 450°F. Coat a rimmed baking sheet with ½ tablespoon oil, then add the radishes, cut sides down, and drizzle with ½ tablespoon oil. Roast for 8 minutes. Scatter the sliced garlic over the radishes, rotate the baking sheet and roast until the bottoms of the radishes are golden brown, 6 to 8 minutes more.

2. While the radishes are roasting, brush the bread with the remaining ½ tablespoon oil; add to the oven along with the radishes and toast until golden brown and crisp. Remove from the oven and rub with the remaining 1 clove garlic.

3. When the radishes are done, toss with the parsley and ¼ teaspoon each salt and pepper, then fold in 1 cup reserved radish leaves. Spoon over the garlic toasts and cut into pieces.

Serves 2
About 225 calories, 11.5 g fat (1.5 g saturated fat), 5 g protein, 540 mg sodium, 26 g carbohydrates, 4 g fiber

Fiery Feta

This "campfire" version of fondue is as delicious as it is easy to clean up afterward (just turn off the grill and toss the foil in the trash).

Active Time 5 minutes | **Total Time** 10 minutes

4 ounces feta
½ red chile, thinly sliced
2 sprigs fresh thyme
4 slices lemon
1 teaspoon honey
1 tablespoon olive oil
Grilled bread, for serving

Heat a grill to medium. Put the feta on a piece of aluminum foil and top with the chile, thyme, lemon, honey and oil. Close the foil and seal. Grill, covered, until warmed through, about 5 minutes. Serve with grilled bread for dunking.

Serves 2
About 230 calories, 19 g fat (9.5 g saturated fat), 8.4 g protein, 520 mg sodium, 7.4 g carbohydrates, 0.9 g fiber

For Brunch Lovers

Who says brunch is exclusively a morning event? Not you!
Indulge in the weekend's most popular cocktail at any time of day.
Appreciate the drink with a batch of a.m. pleasers.

Spicy Bloody Mary

This popular brunch beverage has nursed (or caused!) many a hangover. Ditch the store-bought mixes for a combination of tomato juice, fresh horseradish, celery seed, a dash of hot sauce and plenty of lemon juice. Add pickled pepperoncini brine for a salty and slightly spicy bite.

Active Time 15 minutes | **Total Time** 15 minutes

2 tablespoons fresh lemon juice, plus lemon wedges for serving

½ tablespoon prepared horseradish, squeezed dry

½ teaspoon Tabasco or other hot sauce

½ teaspoon Worcestershire sauce

⅛ teaspoon celery seeds

2 small pepperoncini peppers plus ¾ teaspoon brine

Kosher salt and pepper

¾ cup tomato juice

¼ cup vodka

½ small seedless cucumber, cut into sticks

Celery salt, for serving

1. In a large measuring cup or pitcher, combine the lemon juice, horseradish, hot sauce, Worcestershire sauce, celery seeds, pepperoncini brine and a pinch each of salt and pepper. Stir in the tomato juice and vodka.

2. Rub the rims of two glasses with lemon wedges and dip in the celery salt. Fill the glasses with ice, pour in the drinks, and garnish with cucumber sticks, pepperoncini and lemon wedges.

Serves 2
About 100 calories, 0 g fat (0 g saturated fat), 1.4 g protein, 1,685 mg sodium, 7.4 g carbohydrates, 1.5 g fiber

TEST KITCHEN TIP

If using a spicy vodka, such as one infused with chiles, omit the hot sauce initially, then try a sip and adjust the spiciness with hot sauce as desired.

Mint-Pesto Baked Eggs

Invest in a few pretty ramekins, and it'll be easier than ever to upgrade your morning eggs: Just add the eggs and cream to each ramekin, then top with a bright and flavorful homemade pesto.

Active Time 25 minutes | **Total Time** 40 minutes

3 tablespoons olive oil, plus more for ramekins

⅓ cup packed fresh cilantro leaves

3 tablespoons packed fresh mint leaves

3 tablespoons shelled pistachios

1 small jalapeño, seeded and chopped

2 teaspoons fresh lemon juice

½ small clove garlic

Kosher salt

4 tablespoons heavy cream

4 large eggs

Toasted bread slices, for serving

1. Heat the oven to 425°F. Oil two 10- to 12-ounce ramekins; place on a rimmed baking sheet.

2. In a food processor, pulse the cilantro, mint, pistachios, jalapeño, lemon juice and garlic and a pinch of salt until finely chopped, stopping and stirring occasionally. Pulse in the oil until well combined.

3. To each ramekin, add 2 tablespoons cream and 2 eggs. Top with 1 tablespoon herb mixture and bake until the whites are set but the yolks are still runny, 12 to 15 minutes. Serve with the remaining herb mixture and toasted bread.

Serves 2
About 320 calories, 28 g fat (11 g saturated fat), 14 g protein, 215 mg sodium, 3 g carbohydrates, 1 g fiber

Crispy Egg Toasts, 3 Ways

Fried eggs and toast become elegant when topped with fresh herbs, oils and spices. Start with a foolproof method for cooking crispy fried eggs, then go ahead and upgrade the simple dish and play with other flavors.

PERFECT FRIED EGGS

Active Time 5 minutes | **Total Time** 5 minutes

2 large eggs
3 tablespoons olive oil
   Kosher salt and pepper

Crack 1 egg into each of 2 small cups. Heat the oil in a 10-inch nonstick skillet on medium-high until very hot. Carefully add the eggs; stand back, as the oil will sputter. Cook until the whites are golden brown and crisp around the edges and set around the yolks, about 2 minutes. If the edges are dark but the whites are not set, remove the skillet from the heat; cover for 10 seconds or until the whites are cooked. Season with a pinch each of salt and pepper.

Serves 2
*About 110 calories, 9 g fat (2 g saturated fat), 6.3 g protein,
130 mg sodium, 0.5 g carbohydrates, 0 g fiber*

BASIL-ARUGULA TOASTS

Active Time 10 minutes
Total Time 10 minutes

- ½ cup plus 3 tablespoons olive oil, divided
- ¼ cup chopped fresh basil
- 2 large eggs
  Kosher salt and pepper
- 2 slices bread
  Arugula, for serving
  Crumbled goat cheese, for serving
  Perfect Fried Eggs

1. In a blender, combine ½ cup oil and the basil and set aside.

2. Toast the bread. Top each bread slice with arugula, crumbled goat cheese and a fried egg. Drizzle with some of the basil oil.

Serves 2
About 320 calories, 25.5 g fat (5.5 g saturated fat), 11.1 g protein, 260 mg sodium, 12.1 g carbohydrates, 2.3 g fiber

USE IT UP GOAT CHEESE

Shape the remaining **goat cheese** into a log, then evenly coat the outside with a mix of **grated lemon zest, chopped fresh herbs** and **chopped pink peppercorns**. Drizzle with *olive oil* and **fresh lemon juice** and serve with **baguette slices** or **crackers**.

CURRY-AVOCADO TOASTS

Active Time 10 minutes
Total Time 10 minutes

- ½ teaspoon curry powder
- 5 tablespoons olive oil, divided
- 2 large eggs
  Kosher salt and pepper
- 1 avocado
- 2 teaspoons fresh lime juice
- 2 slices bread
  Perfect Fried Eggs
  Chopped fresh cilantro, for serving

1. In a small dry skillet on medium, toast the curry powder until fragrant, 1 minute. Stir into 2 tablespoons oil and set aside.

2. Mash the avocado with the lime juice and ¼ teaspoon salt. Toast the bread. Top each slice with the avocado mash, a fried egg and cilantro. Drizzle with the curry oil.

Serves 2
About 465 calories, 38.5 g fat (6.5 g saturated fat), 12 g protein, 475 mg sodium, 21.2 g carbohydrates, 9 g fiber

SMOKY RED PEPPER TOASTS

Active Time 10 minutes
Total Time 10 minutes

- ½ teaspoon smoked paprika
- 5 tablespoons olive oil, divided
- 2 large eggs
  Kosher salt and pepper
- 2 slices bread
  Roasted red pepper hummus, for serving
  Perfect Fried Eggs

1. In a small dry skillet on medium, toast the smoked paprika until fragrant, 1 minute. Stir into 2 tablespoons olive oil and set aside.

2. Toast the bread. Top slices with hummus and a crispy egg. Drizzle with the smoked paprika oil.

Serves 2
About 370 calories, 29 g fat (5 g saturated fat), 11.8 g protein, 355 mg sodium, 16 g carbohydrates, 3.2 g fiber

Twice-Baked Citrus Almond Brioche

Bostock, a French pastry that uses day-old brioche, is a brilliant way to reinvent leftover bread for breakfast. Semi-stale slices of brioche are brushed with orange syrup, topped with a homemade almond paste and baked until caramelized.

Active Time 30 minutes | **Total Time** 55 minutes

¾ cup sliced almonds, divided

4 tablespoons sugar, divided

Kosher salt

1 large egg yolk

2 tablespoons unsalted butter, at room temperature

⅛ teaspoon almond extract

½ tablespoon grated orange zest plus 2 tablespoons orange juice

½ tablespoon olive oil

½ tablespoon fresh thyme leaves

3 ¾-inch-thick slices brioche

Sliced citrus, for serving

1. Heat the oven to 400°F. In a mini food processor, pulse ¼ cup almonds, 2 tablespoons sugar and a pinch of salt until finely ground. Add the egg yolk and butter; process to form a paste. Add the almond extract; pulse to combine.

2. In a small saucepan, simmer the orange zest and juice, 2 tablespoons water and the remaining 2 tablespoons sugar on medium-high, stirring, until the sugar dissolves. Remove from the heat; let the syrup cool.

3. In a small bowl, combine the oil and thyme, the remaining ½ cup almonds and a pinch of salt.

4. Arrange the bread on a baking sheet. Brush each slice with the syrup until very moist, then spread with an even layer of almond paste (about 2 heaping tablespoons on each slice). Top with the almond-thyme mixture.

5. Bake until the toasts are caramelized on the edges and the almonds are golden brown, 20 to 25 minutes. Serve with the citrus and additional orange syrup if desired.

Serves 2
About 420 calories, 24 g fat (7 g saturated fat), 9 g protein, 230 mg sodium, 46 g carbohydrates, 4 g fiber

Raspberry "Cheesecake" French Toast

Nothing screams "celebration" like serving up a dessert-like treat for breakfast. While this dish is technically breakfast (hello, French toast!), it's stuffed with a creamy berry-studded filling, drizzled with syrup and dusted with confectioners' sugar.

Active Time 20 minutes | **Total Time** 20 minutes

3 ounces cream cheese, at room temperature

½ teaspoon vanilla extract

1½ tablespoons raspberry jam

¼ cup milk

1 large egg

⅛ teaspoon ground cinnamon

4 ½-inch-thick slices brioche

¼ cup raspberries, plus more for serving

Nonstick cooking spray, for the pan

Confectioners' sugar and maple syrup, for serving

1. Using an electric mixer, beat the cream cheese with the vanilla in a medium bowl on medium speed until smooth. Stir in the jam. In a shallow dish, whisk the milk, egg and cinnamon.

2. Spread the cheese mixture on one side of the brioche slices. Divide the raspberries between 2 of the slices; top with the remaining slices, pressing to make 4 sandwiches.

3. Heat a 12-inch nonstick skillet on medium; spray with nonstick cooking spray. Dip the sandwiches into the egg mixture, turning to soak both sides. Place the sandwiches in the skillet; cook until golden brown, 2 to 3 minutes per side.

4. Dust with confectioners' sugar. Serve with maple syrup and more raspberries.

Serves 2
About 340 calories, 20 g fat (11 g saturated fat), 8 g protein, 325 mg sodium, 33 g carbohydrates, 3 g fiber

---

SWITCH IT UP

Swap in different fruits or jams to transform this dish into something new.

DOUBLE BERRY Berry jam + fresh blueberries

MELBA Peach jam + fresh raspberries

VIP Pool Party

With these recipes you have tickets for the summer's hottest event—a poolside lounge. (If you don't have a pool, throw on a bathing suit and pretend!) Fruit-infused vodka drinks and skewer snacks will keep you feeling refreshed and cool.

BLACKBERRY-MINT MULE

Active Time 10 minutes
Total Time 10 minutes

  3 ounces blackberries, plus more for serving
¼ cup fresh mint, plus more for serving
  4 ounces vodka
  1 ounce lime juice
  1 lime, sliced
  6 ounces ginger beer

In a pitcher, smash the blackberries and mint. Stir in the vodka, lime juice and sliced lime. Gently stir in the ginger beer. Serve over ice with extra blackberries and mint.

Serves 2
About 220 calories, 0.5 g fat (0 g saturated fat), 1.3 g protein, 5 mg sodium, 23.4 g carbohydrates, 4.9 g fiber

THYME-PLUM MULE

Active Time 10 minutes
Total Time 10 minutes

  4 ounces vodka
  1 ounce lime juice
  1 plum, thinly sliced, plus more for serving
  4 sprigs fresh thyme, plus more for serving
  6 ounces ginger beer

In a pitcher, stir together the vodka, lime juice, sliced plum and thyme. Gently stir in the ginger beer. Serve over ice with extra sliced plums and thyme.

Serves 2
About 210 calories, 0 g fat (0 g saturated fat), 0.5 g protein, 0 mg sodium, 20.8 g carbohydrates, 1 g fiber

TEST KITCHEN TIP

The copper mug is almost as essential to this ice-cold vodka drink as the lime and ginger beer. Place the mugs in the freezer until frosty (about 20 minutes) before serving so the drinks will stay cooler longer.

Peach & Prosciutto Skewers

The hardest part about making these appetizers is waiting for the mozzarella to marinate.

Active Time 20 minutes | **Total Time** 15 minutes plus marinating

¼ cup olive oil

1 tablespoon red wine vinegar

1 tablespoon chopped fresh herbs (like basil, thyme and oregano)

⅛ teaspoon red pepper flakes

Kosher salt

5 ounces bocconcini mozzarella (about 8 balls)

4 slices prosciutto

1 peach or nectarine, cut into 8 wedges

1. In a medium bowl, whisk together the oil, vinegar, herbs and red pepper flakes and ¼ teaspoon salt. Add the mozzarella and turn to coat. Let sit at room temperature 1 hour or refrigerate overnight.

2. When ready to serve, remove the mozzarella from the marinade. Cut the prosciutto slices in half lengthwise and fold accordion-style. Slide onto the bamboo skewers with the mozzarella and peach wedges.

Serves 2
About 430 calories, 33 g fat (16.5 g saturated fat), 26.2 g protein, 780 mg sodium, 7.2 g carbohydrates, 1.1 g fiber

Game Day Grub

No, you don't need a crowd to cheer on your favorite sports teams! Score big with these scaled-down versions of tailgate greats, perfect with an ice cold beer or hard seltzer.

Avocado Dip

While guac may be everyone's go-to, it's not the *only* way to serve up avocado in dip form. Char up vegetables, then throw everything into a blender to make this creamy, dairy-free dip.

Active Time 30 minutes | **Total Time** 30 minutes | **Makes** about 1 cup

1 small poblano pepper

1 clove garlic, not peeled

½ jalapeño

½ small onion, halved

1 tablespoon olive oil

1 ripe avocado

½ bunch cilantro, including stems

2 to 3 tablespoon fresh lime juice (from 1 to 2 limes)

Kosher salt

Totchos, for serving

1. Heat broiler. On a small rimmed baking sheet, toss poblano, garlic, jalapeño and onion with oil. Broil, turning vegetables once halfway through, until deeply charred, 6 to 8 minutes. Let cool, then use a paper towel to remove any skins and seeds.

2. Transfer vegetables to a blender along with avocado, cilantro, 2 tablespoons lime juice, 1 tablespoon water and ¼ tsp salt and puree until smooth, adding 1 to 2 tablespoons more lime juice or water as needed. Serve with Totchos if desired.

Per Serving (⅓ cup)
70 calories, 6 g fat (1 g saturted), 1 g protein, 85 mg sodium, 5 g carbohydrates, 3 g fiber

---

TOTCHOS

Heat oven to 425°F. On a large rimmed baking sheet, toss **½ pound potato tots** with **1 teaspoon oil**, **½ teaspoon chili powder**, **¼ teaspoon ground cumin**, **¼ teaspoon ground coriander** and a **pinch of cayenne** and roast 20 minutes. Sprinkle with **¼ cup finely grated extra-sharp Cheddar cheese** and roast until tots are golden brown and cheese has melted, 6 to 8 minutes.

French Onion Dip

No soup mix here! Caramelizing onions takes some time, but the sweet and rich results really make it worthwhile. Good news: This dish will last in the fridge for up to a week.

Active Time 55 minutes | **Total Time** 1 hour plus standing
Makes 3 ½ cups

2 tablespoons unsalted butter

3 large onions, thinly sliced

   Kosher salt and pepper

1 tablespoon fresh thyme leaves

¼ cup dry sherry wine

8 ounces crème fraîche

½ cup full-fat Greek yogurt

1 tablespoon grated lemon zest

¼ cup chopped fresh chives

   Baguette, sliced and toasted, for serving

1. Melt butter in a large skillet on medium-low. Add onions, season with ½ teaspoon salt and ¼ teaspoon pepper and cook, covered, stirring occasionally, until tender, 8 to 10 minutes.

2. Increase heat to medium and cook, stirring frequently, until deep golden brown, 30 to 40 minutes. (Add 1 to 2 tablespoons water if onions stick or pan browns.) Stir in thyme and cook 1 minute. Stir in sherry and simmer until evaporated. Let cool.

3. Mix in crème fraîche, yogurt and lemon zest until smooth. Fold in all but 1 tablespoon chives. Let stand 30 minutes to allow flavors to meld before serving.

4. Sprinkle with remaining chives and serve with toasted baguette.

Per Serving (¼ cup)
About 100 calories, 8.5 g fat (5.5 g saturated), 2 g protein, 85 mg sodium, 4 g carbohydrates, 1 g fiber

TEST KITCHEN TIP

To reheat leftovers, microwave on Medium or bake in a 375°F oven until soft and delicious.

Buffalo Chicken Dip

Wings can be messy, especially when they're doused in hot sauce and served with a cool dipping sauce. Try turning the fan-favorite fare into a super-satisfying dip for all the deliciousness mess-free!

Active Time 20 minutes | **Total Time** 35 minutes | **Makes** 6 servings

4 ounces cream cheese, at room temp

¼ cup sour cream

1 tablespoon fresh lemon juice

3 tablespoon Buffalo-style hot sauce (we used Frank's Red Hot)

1 ½ cups finely shredded white-meat rotisserie chicken (from 1 chicken)

4 ounces Monterey Jack cheese, coarsely grated

1 scallion, finely chopped

1 ounces blue cheese, crumbled

Potato chips and celery sticks, for serving

1. Heat oven to 425°F. In a bowl, whisk cream cheese, sour cream, lemon juice and hot sauce. Fold in chicken, Monterey Jack and scallions.

2. Transfer mixture to two 8-ounce ramekins, top with blue cheese and bake until golden brown, 12 to 15 minutes. Serve with potato chips and celery sticks.

Per Serving (⅓ cup)
About 215 calories, 16.5 g fat (9.5 g saturated), 15 g protein, 505 mg sodium, 3 g carbohydrates, 0 g fiber

TEST KITCHEN TIP

Keep leftover dip in the fridge for up to 1 week. To reheat, microwave on Medium or bake in a 375°F oven, covered with foil, until warm.

Vegan Queso

Ooey-gooey goodness without an ounce of dairy! The secret? Cashews and nutritional yeast work as a delicious (surprising!) replacement for cheese.

Active Time 30 minutes | **Total Time** 45 minutes | **Makes** about 1 cup

1 large poblano pepper, halved and seeded

1 tablespoon olive oil

1 clove garlic, pressed

1/2 cup cashews

1 teaspoon chili powder

1/2 teaspoon ground cumin

1/4 teaspoon ground coriander

1/4 teaspoon ground turmeric

Kosher salt and pepper

2 tablespoons nutritional yeast

Chopped cilantro and tortilla chips, for serving

1. Heat broiler. Arrange poblano, cut sides down, on a small rimmed baking sheet and broil until charred, 3 to 5 minutes. Transfer to a bowl, cover and let stand 5 minutes. Use a paper towel to remove skins, then cut pepper into 1/4-inch pieces.

2. Meanwhile, heat oil and garlic in a small saucepan on medium until sizzling, about 1 minute. Remove from heat and stir in cashews, then spices and 1/4 teaspoon each salt and pepper. Add 3/4 cup water and bring mixture to a boil. Reduce heat and simmer until cashews are tender, 10 to 12 minutes.

3. Transfer mixture to blender, add nutritional yeast and 1/4 cup water and puree until smooth.

4. Return mixture to saucepan and cook, stirring occasionally, until thickened, 6 to 8 minutes. Fold in all but 1 tablespoon poblanos. Transfer to serving dish, top with remaining poblanos and sprinkle with cilantro. Serve with tortilla chips.

Per Serving (1/4 cup)
About 140 calories, 10 g fat (2 g saturated), 5 g protein, 150 mg sodium, 9 g carbohydrates, 2 g fiber

STRAWBERRY-RHUBARB
CRUMBLES PG. 205

Chapter 7

Small-Batch Desserts

Many dessert recipes leave you with 24 or 48 brownies, cookies or bars. While this is great for sharing with others, it's not ideal for a household of two. Enter these scaled-down versions of your favorite sweets. Now you can satisfy your craving and whip up freshly baked cake, cookies, brownies, pies and more.

Molten Chocolate Skillet Brownies

Forget the box and bake up two perfectly portioned homemade brownies. These are made in mini skillets, so you can easily top them with a scoop of ice cream, grab a spoon and dig into the chocolatey goodness.

Active Time 25 minutes | **Total Time** 40 minutes | **Makes** 2

¼ cup (½ stick) unsalted butter, cut up, plus more for the skillets

4 ounces dark chocolate (50% to 65% cacao), finely chopped

2 large eggs, separated

1 tablespoon unsweetened cocoa powder

½ teaspoon pure vanilla extract

¼ teaspoon kosher salt

⅓ cup sugar

Raspberries and vanilla ice cream, for serving (optional)

1. Heat the oven to 350°F. Butter two mini (6- to 6 ½-inch) cast-iron skillets; place on a baking sheet. In a medium bowl, microwave the butter and chocolate on High in 30-second intervals, stirring in between, until the chocolate has melted. Stir the mixture until smooth; set aside.

2. In a medium bowl, whisk the egg yolks, cocoa powder, vanilla and salt and half the sugar until smooth; whisk into the chocolate mixture.

3. Using an electric mixer, beat the egg whites on medium-high speed until soft peaks form, about 3 minutes. With the mixer running, gradually add the remaining sugar, beating until stiff peaks form. Stir one-fourth of the beaten whites into the chocolate mixture until combined. In two batches, gently fold the remaining whites into the chocolate mixture without deflating the whites.

4. Divide the batter between the skillets; transfer the baking sheet with the skillets to the oven and bake until puffed, 15 to 18 minutes. Let stand for 10 minutes. Serve warm with raspberries and ice cream if desired.

Per Serving (1 brownie)
About 740 calories, 50 g fat (28 g saturated fat), 10 g protein, 380 mg sodium, 66 g carbohydrates, 6 g fiber

SMALL-BATCH BROWNIES

Looking for square brownies instead? Use a loaf pan! In step 4, transfer the batter to a greased 8 ½- by 4 ½-inch loaf pan, then bake until a toothpick inserted in the center comes out clean, 28 to 30 minutes. Let stand before cutting and serving.

Mug Cakes

Satisfy any cake craving with the laziest, most delicious recipe, ready in 10 minutes or less: Mix and microwave a personal dessert right in your mug!

Red Velvet Mug Cake

This boldly colored beauty features a gooey cream cheese frosting hidden in the center.

Active Time 10 minutes | **Total Time** 10 minutes

- ¼ cup plus 2 tablespoons all-purpose flour
- 2 tablespoons granulated sugar
- 1 teaspoon unsweetened cocoa powder
- ¼ teaspoon baking powder
- ⅛ teaspoon kosher salt
- ⅓ cup whole milk
- 2 tablespoons unsalted butter, melted
- 2 teaspoons pure vanilla extract
- 1 teaspoon red food coloring
- 3 tablespoons confectioners' sugar
- 1 tablespoon cream cheese, at room temperature

In a 12-ounce mug, whisk together the flour, granulated sugar, cocoa powder, baking powder and salt. Stir in the milk, butter, vanilla and food coloring. In a small bowl, mix together the confectioners' sugar and cream cheese until smooth, then drop into the mug and push down until covered by the batter. Microwave on High until just cooked through, about 1 ½ minutes.

Serves 1

About 690 calories, 31.5 g fat (19 g saturated fat), 8.9 g protein, 465 mg sodium, 90.6 g carbohydrates, 1.9 g fiber

Chocolate Mug Cake

Turn the flavors of turtle candies into a rich chocolate cake dotted with toasted pecans and melty caramels.

Active Time 10 minutes | **Total Time** 10 minutes

- ¼ cup all-purpose flour
- 2 tablespoons granulated sugar
- 2 tablespoons unsweetened cocoa powder
- ¼ teaspoon baking powder
- ⅛ teaspoon kosher salt
- ⅓ cup whole milk
- 2 tablespoons unsalted butter, melted
- 2 teaspoons pure vanilla extract
- 4 squares caramel, quartered
- ¼ cup toasted pecans, chopped

In a 12-ounce mug, whisk together the flour, sugar, cocoa powder, baking powder and salt. Stir in the milk, butter and vanilla. Fold in the caramel and pecans. Microwave on High until just cooked through, about 1 ½ minutes.

Serves 1

About 880 calories, 55 g fat (23 g saturated fat), 10.6 g protein, 485 mg sodium, 92.3 g carbohydrates, 7.4 g fiber

Blueberry-Lemon Mug Cake

The berries burst when heated, creating juicy pockets of goodness in a zesty citrus cake.

Active Time 10 minutes | **Total Time** 5 minutes

- ½ cup all-purpose flour
- 2 tablespoons granulated sugar
- ¼ teaspoon baking powder
- ⅛ teaspoon kosher salt
- ⅓ cup whole milk
- 2 tablespoons unsalted butter, melted
- 2 teaspoons pure vanilla extract
- 1 teaspoon grated lemon zest
- ¼ cup fresh or frozen blueberries (frozen blueberries retain their shape better than fresh ones)

In a 12-ounce mug, whisk together the flour, sugar, baking powder and salt. Stir in the milk, butter, vanilla and lemon zest. Fold in the blueberries. Microwave on High until just cooked through, about 1 ½ to 2 minutes.

Serves 1

About 515 calories, 26 g fat (16 g saturated fat), 6.2 g protein, 420 mg sodium, 59.4 g carbohydrates, 2.1 g fiber

Pumpkin Spice Cupcakes with Cream Cheese Frosting

Whether it's peak PSL season or the middle of July, these cupcakes bring a dose of warmth and comfort.

Active Time 30 minutes | **Total Time** 1 hour | **Makes** 6

- ¾ cup all-purpose flour
- ¾ teaspoon pumpkin pie spice
- ½ teaspoon baking powder
- ¼ teaspoon baking soda
- ⅛ teaspoon kosher salt
- ½ cup canned pure pumpkin puree
- 1 tablespoon molasses (not blackstrap)
- ½ teaspoon pure vanilla extract
- ¼ cup (½ stick) unsalted butter, at room temperature
- ¼ cup plus 2 tablespoons sugar
- 1 large egg
- 2 ounces cream cheese, at room temperature
- 1 tablespoon unsalted butter, at room temperature
- 1 cup confectioners' sugar
- ½ teaspoon vanilla extract

1. Heat the oven to 350°F. Line a 6-cup muffin pan with paper liners or place 6 liners in a 12-cup muffin pan, spacing them out evenly.

2. In a medium bowl, whisk the flour, pumpkin pie spice, baking powder, baking soda and salt; set aside.

3. In another bowl, combine the pumpkin, molasses and vanilla.

4. Using an electric mixer, beat the butter and granulated sugar on medium speed until light and fluffy, about 3 minutes. Beat in the egg. Reduce the speed to low and alternately add the flour mixture and the pumpkin mixture, mixing just until incorporated.

5. Divide the batter among the muffin-pan cups (heaping ¼ cup each) and bake until a toothpick inserted into the center comes out clean, 18 to 25 minutes. Transfer to a wire rack; let cool for 5 minutes before removing the cupcakes from the pan to cool completely.

6. In a medium bowl, using an electric mixer, beat the cream cheese and butter until light and fluffy, about 3 minutes. Gradually beat in the confectioners' sugar and vanilla until light and fluffy, 2 minutes. Spread the frosting on top of the cooled cupcakes.

Per Serving (1 cupcake)
About 335 calories, 14 g fat (8 g saturated fat), 4 g protein, 200 mg sodium, 50 g carbohydrates, 1 g fiber

---

USE IT UP PUMPKIN PUREE

Save in the fridge for a couple of days: Stir into espresso and steamed milk (with sugar and spices), fold into pancake batter and sub for tomato sauce to top a homemade pizza.

Roasted Apples

Satisfy those sugar cravings with a fiber- and antioxidant-filled treat that will make the doctor (and you!) very happy. you If you want to indulge, swap out the yogurt for vanilla ice cream or a drizzle of caramel.

Active Time 5 minutes | **Total Time** 20 minutes

1 tablespoon olive oil

2 apples, halved and cored

4 sprigs fresh thyme, plus more for serving

Vanilla Greek yogurt, for serving

1. Heat the oven to 425°F. Coat a small rimmed baking sheet with olive oil. Place the apples, cut sides down, on the baking sheet, then sprinkle with thyme and roast until tender, 15 to 18 minutes.

2. Place the apples in bowls, cut sides up, and add dollops of yogurt. Spoon any pan juices on top and sprinkle with additional thyme if desired.

Serves 2
About 155 calories, 6 g fat (1 g saturated fat), 2 g protein, 10 mg sodium, 27 g carbohydrates, 4 g fiber

PEACHES WITH HONEY AND PISTACHIOS

Grill **2 peaches** (halved), cut sides down, until slightly charred and caramelized, 1 to 2 minutes. Turn and cook, with the grill or grill pan covered, for 2 minutes more. In a bowl, combine **¼ cup plain Greek yogurt** and **¼ teaspoon grated orange zest**. Transfer the peaches to plates and spoon the yogurt on top, then drizzle with **1 tablespoon honey** and sprinkle with **2 tablespoons chopped pistachios** and **fresh mint leaves**.

Strawberry-Rhubarb Crumbles

Mini skillets make it easy to enjoy a fruity dessert without the need to share. You can use shallow casserole dishes, but the timing might be a different, so watch them carefully. (See photo on page 196.)

Active Time 20 minutes | **Total Time** 1 hour | **Makes** 2

3 tablespoons cold unsalted butter, cut into small pieces, plus more for the skillets

6 ounces strawberries, halved (quartered if large)

6 ounces rhubarb, trimmed and cut into ½-inch pieces

½ tablespoon cornstarch

3 ½ tablespoons sugar, divided

¼ cup plus 2 tablespoons all-purpose flour

⅛ teaspoon kosher salt

2 tablespoons unsalted almonds, roughly chopped

Vanilla ice cream, for serving (optional)

1. Heat the oven to 425°F. Line a baking sheet with parchment paper. Lightly butter two mini (6- to 6 ½-inch) cast-iron skillets and place on the prepared sheet.

2. In a large bowl, toss together the strawberries, rhubarb and cornstarch and 2 tablespoons sugar.

3. In a second bowl, use your hands to rub the butter and flour together to resemble breadcrumbs. Add the salt, the almonds and the remaining 1 ½ tablespoons sugar and squeeze the mixture together with your fingertips to form small clumps.

4. Divide the fruit mixture between the prepared skillets and top with the crumble mixture (they will appear overfilled). Bake until bubbling and the tops are golden brown, 30 to 35 minutes. Serve with ice cream if desired.

Serves 2
About 440 calories, 24 g fat (12.5 g saturated fat), 5.6 g protein, 125 mg sodium, 52.7 g carbohydrates, 4.5 g fiber

---

SWITCH IT UP

Rhubarb and strawberries not in season? Swap in a different fruit! Use **6 ounces of pears** (sliced) and **6 ounces of blackberries**, then bake for 35 to 45 minutes. Or, use **6 ounces of blueberries** and **6 ounces of strawberries** (halved) and bake for 35 to 45 minutes.

TOP IT OFF

"MAGIC" CHOCOLATE SAUCE In a small bowl, microwave **2 ounces good-quality semisweet (50% to 65% cacao) chocolate**, chopped, and **3 tablespoons refined coconut oil** on High in 20-second intervals until melted, stirring in between. Cool completely before pouring over the bananas. If necessary, reheat for 10 to 20 seconds to remelt to pouring consistency. Store in an airtight container at room temperature for up to 2 weeks.

CARAMEL SAUCE In a small saucepan with a candy thermometer attached, stir together **1/2 cup sugar, 2 tablespoons water** and **1/2 tablespoon light corn syrup.** Heat to boiling on medium-high without stirring, about 1 to 3 minutes, then boil until dark amber (320°F to 345°F on a candy thermometer), 5 to 9 minutes. Quickly remove the pan from the heat and stir in **1/4 cup warmed heavy cream** and **2 tablespoons unsalted butter**, stirring until smooth. Let the caramel cool slightly, then stir in **1/4 teaspoon vanilla extract** and **1/8 teaspoon kosher salt** and cool completely. Store in an airtight container at room temperature up to 1 month. Reheat in the microwave before serving.

Chocolate-Covered Banana "Ice Cream" Sundaes

When frozen and blended in a food processor, bananas turn into a creamy, dairy-free soft-serve, sometimes called "nice cream." Serve it up with melted dark chocolate and a cherry on top, or give one of these other toppings a try—if you use plant-based semisweet chocolate, the "Magic" Chocolate Sauce topping is vegan too!

Active Time 5 minutes | **Total Time** 5 minutes

2 large ripe bananas

1 ounce plant-based dark chocolate (60% to 70% cacao)

2 cherries

1. Peel and slice the bananas, then freeze until firm, 3 hours.

2. Pulse the frozen bananas in a food processor, scraping down the sides of the bowl often.

3. Microwave the chocolate on High in 30-second intervals, stirring in between, until melted and smooth.

4. Divide the bananas between two bowls, drizzle with the chocolate and top each with 1 cherry.

Serves 2
About 205 calories, 6 g fat (3 g saturated fat), 2 g protein, 2 mg sodium, 40 g carbohydrates, 5 g fiber

Honey-Peach Margarita Sorbet

Mix up a batch of margaritas to enjoy on the rocks, then add a splash of your drink to this zesty, fruity sorbet for a icy, refreshing treat. (Store-bought margarita mix can work here too in a pinch.)

Active Time 5 minutes | **Total Time** 5 minutes

    1 pound frozen peaches, slightly thawed
    3 tablespoons Classic Margarita (page 161)
    2 tablespoons honey
    ¼ teaspoon vanilla extract
      Pinch of kosher salt

In a food processor, puree the peaches, margarita, honey, vanilla and salt until smooth. Serve immediately or transfer to a loaf pan and freeze until ready to serve.

Serves 2
About 195 calories, 0 g fat (0 g saturated fat), 1.6 g protein, 60 mg sodium, 42.6 g carbohydrates, 3.1 g fiber

Avocado Mousse

This velvety, rich no-bake dessert has not a single ounce of cream or milk (the secret: heart-healthy avocado), so it's perfect for anyone looking to avoid dairy.

Active Time 5 minutes | **Total Time** 5 minutes

    1 large ripe avocado, pitted and peeled
    ¼ cup Dutch-process cocoa powder
    3 tablespoons unsweetened almond milk
    2 tablespoons honey or date syrup
    1 teaspoon pure vanilla extract
      Pinch of kosher salt
      Shaved chocolate of choice, for serving

In a mini food processor, puree the avocado, cocoa powder, almond milk, honey, vanilla and salt. Chill if desired. Divide between two small glasses and serve with shaved chocolate.

Serves 2
About 305 calories, 21 g fat (2.5 g saturated fat), 5 g protein, 88 mg sodium, 33 g carbohydrates, 12 g fiber

---

SPIKED BERRY SUNDAE SAUCE

In a bowl, whisk together **1 ½ tablespoons margarita** and **1 tablespoon sugar** to dissolve the sugar. Toss with **8 ounces mixed berries** and let sit, tossing occasionally, at least 20 minutes. Serve over vanilla ice cream. Makes 1 ½ cups.

COCO RAZZ SMOOTHIES

Blend together **1 cup each unsweetened almond milk** and **low-fat coconut-flavored yogurt** with **4 cups frozen raspberries** and **4 bananas**, peeled and cut into pieces. Divide between two glasses and serve topped with **toasted coconut** and **raspberries**.

Freeze-and-Bake Chocolate Chip Cookies

Spend a few minutes making this dough to stash in your freezer so you'll have proportioned cookie dough ready whenever a craving strikes. Just pop one or two onto a small baking sheet in your toaster oven and bake for an ooey-gooey treat.

Active Time 20 minutes | **Total Time** 35 minutes plus freezing | **Makes** 12

2 cups all-purpose flour

1 teaspoon baking soda

½ teaspoon kosher salt

1 cup plant-based dark chocolate chips

1 cup plant-based semisweet chocolate chips

½ cup firmly packed dark brown sugar

½ cup granulated sugar

½ cup canola oil

2 teaspoons pure vanilla extract

1. In a medium bowl, whisk together the flour, baking soda and salt. Toss with the chocolate chips; set aside.

2. In a second bowl, break up the brown sugar, making sure there are no lumps. Add the granulated sugar, the oil, ¼ cup water and the vanilla and whisk to combine. Add the flour mixture and mix until just combined (there should be no streaks of flour).

3. Line a cookie sheet with parchment paper. Spoon out ¼-cupfuls of dough into mounds on the sheet, gently gathering dough together with your hands without pressing. (Dough will be crumbly.) Freeze for 30 minutes, until solid. Transfer to a freezer-safe airtight container or resealable plastic bag, labeled with the date, and store in the freezer for up to 3 months.

4. When ready to bake, heat the oven or a toaster oven to 375°F. Line a small baking sheet or the toaster oven tray with parchment paper and place 1 or 2 frozen cookie dough mounds (at least 2 inches apart if more than 1) on the sheet. Bake until the edges are golden brown, 10 to 13 minutes total, rotating the pan halfway through for even baking. Let cool completely on the pan on a wire rack.

Per Serving (1 cookie)
About 400 calories, 20.5 g fat (7 g saturated fat), 4 g protein, 190 mg sodium, 50 g carbohydrates, 1 g fiber

Raspberry-Cranberry Hand Pies

When you want a flaky crust with a tart fruity filling but don't want to deal with leftovers, embrace the hand pie.

Active Time 15 minutes | **Total Time** 30 minutes plus chilling | **Makes** 6

1 ¼ cups all-purpose flour

1 tablespoon granulated sugar

½ teaspoon kosher salt

½ cup (1 stick) cold unsalted butter, cut into small pieces

3 to 4 tablespoons ice water

3 ounces fresh raspberries, halved if large

¼ cup whole-berry cranberry sauce

½ teaspoon cornstarch

1 large egg, beaten

Granulated sugar, for sprinkling

¼ cup confectioners' sugar, for glaze (optional)

1. In a food processor, combine the flour, sugar and salt. Add the butter and pulse until the mixture resembles pea-size crumbs. Add 3 tablespoons ice water, pulsing until the dough forms small clumps and holds together when squeezed (if necessary, add up to another tablespoon of water, 1 teaspoon at a time). Do not overmix.

2. Transfer the dough to a piece of plastic wrap and shape into 2 rectangles. Wrap tightly and refrigerate until firm, at least 1 hour and up to 2 days.

3. Heat the oven to 400°F. Line a baking sheet with parchment paper. Working on a lightly floured surface, roll 1 rectangle of dough to an 11- by 14-inch rectangle (about ¹/₁₆ inch thick). Cut out twelve 2 ½- by 4-inch rectangles, rerolling and cutting scraps as necessary and using the second rectangle of dough as needed. Arrange 6 rectangles on the prepared baking sheet. Using a fork, prick holes in the remaining 6 rectangles.

4. In a bowl, toss the raspberries with the cranberry sauce and cornstarch. Spoon 1 heaping tablespoon cranberry mixture into the center of each rectangle on the sheet, leaving a ½-inch border around the edges. Lightly brush the border with some egg. Top with the prickled rectangles and press the edges with a fork to seal. Refrigerate for 10 minutes.

5. Brush the tops of the hand pies with the remaining egg and sprinkle with granulated sugar. Bake until golden brown, 12 to 15 minutes. Transfer to a wire rack to cool. If desired, whisk the confectioners' sugar with a little cold water until drizzling consistency and drizzle over the tops.

Per Serving (1 hand pie)
About 285 calories, 16.5 g fat (10 g saturated fat), 4 g protein, 175 mg sodium, 31 g carbohydrates, 2 g fiber

Very Berry Quinoa Muffins

Whether you are looking to have a small batch of muffins to serve with brunch or want to have breakfast already made for the next few mornings, this recipe has you covered.

Active Time 10 minutes | **Total Time** 30 minutes | **Makes** 6

Nonstick cooking spray, for the pan

6 tablespoons all-purpose flour, plus more for dusting

1/2 cup almond flour

2 tablespoons white quinoa (raw)

1/2 teaspoon baking powder

1/2 teaspoon ground cinnamon

1/4 teaspoon ground ginger

1/4 teaspoon baking soda

1/4 teaspoon kosher salt

1 large egg, beaten

1/2 cup plain full-fat yogurt

2 tablespoons whole milk

3 tablespoons honey

1 6-ounce container small raspberries

1. Heat oven to 325°F. Lightly coat a 6-cup muffin pan with cooking spray and dust with flour.

2. In a medium bowl, whisk together the flours, quinoa, baking powder, cinnamon, ginger, baking soda and salt.

3. In a small bowl, whisk the egg, yogurt, milk and honey. Fold the egg mixture into the flour mixture until just combined, then stir in the raspberries.

4. Divide the batter among the muffin-pan cups and bake until a toothpick inserted into the center of a muffin comes out clean, 15 to 20 minutes. Cool in the pan for 5 minutes, then transfer to a wire rack to cool completely.

Per Serving (1 muffin)
About 170 calories, 7 g fat (1 g saturated fat), 6 g protein, 205 mg sodium, 23 g carbohydrates, 3 g fiber

Index

HEARST
HOME

Cover and book design by Olivia Alchek and Mike Nicholls

Library of Congress Cataloging-in-Publication Data Available on request

10 9 8 7 6 5 4 3 2 1

Published by Hearst Home, an imprint of Hearst Books/Hearst Communications, Inc.
300 W 57th Street
New York, NY 10019

Good Housekeeping, Hearst Home, the Hearst Home logo, and Hearst Books
are registered trademarks of Hearst Communications, Inc.

For information about custom editions, special sales, premium and corporate purchases:
hearst.com/magazines/hearst-books

Printed in the U.S.A.
ISBN 978-1-950785-83-4

MEAT COOKING CHEAT SHEET

Follow this chart for perfectly cooked protein every time.

MEAT	# OF PIECES	WEIGHT	THICKNESS	SEAR TIME PER SIDE	ROAST TIME
Beef (strip or sirloin steak)	1	1 pound	1 ½ inches	2–3 minutes	5 minutes for medium-rare (135°F)
Chicken (boneless, skinless breasts)	2	1 ½ pounds	1 inch	2–3 minutes	6-8 minutes to cook through (165°F)
Chicken (boneless, skinless thighs)	4	1 ½ pounds	1 inch	1–2 minutes	3 minutes to cook through (165°F)
Chicken (bone-in, skin-on thighs)	4	1 ¾ pounds	1 inch	2–3 minutes	10 minutes to cook through (165°F)
Pork (bone-in center-cut rib chops)	4	2 pounds	1 ¼ inches	2–3 minutes	8 minutes for medium-rare (145°F)

GRAIN CHEAT SHEET

To store, let cooked grains cool completely, then refrigerate in an airtight container for up to 5 days or freeze for up to 1 month.

GRAIN	GRAIN TO LIQUID (CUPS)	STOVETOP INSTRUCTIONS
Brown rice	1:1.75	Bring water and rice to a boil, then cover and simmer on low until water is absorbed and rice is tender, about 35 min. Remove from heat and let stand, covered, 10 min.
Bulgur	1:2	Bring water to a boil, then stir in bulgur. Cover and simmer on low until water is absorbed and bulgur is tender, about 15 min. Remove from heat and let stand, covered, 10 min.
Farro (pearled)	1:8	Bring water to a boil. Add farro and cook, as with pasta, until firm yet tender, about 30 min. Drain.
Quinoa	1:2	Bring water and quinoa to a boil, then cover and simmer on low until water is absorbed and quinoa is tender, about 15 min. Remove from heat and let stand, covered, 5 min.
White rice	1:1.5	Bring water and rice to a boil, then cover and simmer on low until water is absorbed and rice is just tender, 15 min. Remove from heat and let stand, covered, 10 min.

VEGETABLE ROASTING CHEAT SHEET

Heat oven to 450°F. Then proceed with the specific instructions for each vegetable below.

INGREDIENT	PREP	TIME	FLAVORING
Asparagus	Trimmed	8 to 12 minutes	Sprinkle with lemon zest.
Beets (without tops)	Whole, unpeeled, pricked with a fork, then peeled after roasting	1 hour	Peel, cut into pieces and season with salt, pepper and grated orange zest.
Broccoli	Trimmed and stem peeled, florets split into ½-inch-wide pieces	10 to 15 minutes	Sprinkle with grated Parmesan or extra-sharp Cheddar.
Brussels sprouts	Trimmed and halved through stem end	15 to 20 minutes	Toss with maple syrup immediately after roasting.
Butternut squash	Cut into 1-inch pieces	25 to 35 minutes	Toss with fresh thyme before roasting.
Cauliflower	Cut into 1 ½-inch florets	20 to 30 minutes	Sprinkle with chopped fresh parsley and red pepper flakes.
Green beans	Trimmed	10 to 15 minutes	Toss with chopped fresh dill or chives.
Potatoes & sweet potatoes	Cut into 1-inch-thick wedges	25 to 30 minutes	Toss with coriander or fresh rosemary before roasting.
Sweet peppers	Cut into 1-inch-wide strips	15 to 25 minutes	Toss with chopped fresh parsley, a splash of vinegar and salt and pepper.